THE *Blue* BOOK OF BOUNDARIES

SAPPHIRE EDITION

TIFFANY BUCKNER

© 2021, Tiffany Buckner
The Blue Book of Boundaries
www.tiffanybuckner.com
info@anointedfire.com

Published by:
Anointed Fire™ House
www.anointedfirehouse.com

Cover Design by:
Anointed Fire™ House

Author photograph by:
Photo by: Brand You Brand Nu

Edited by:
Jose Juguna

ISBN: 978-1-7354654-7-0

This book contains material protected under International and Federal Copyright Laws and Treaties. Any unauthorized reprint or use of this material is prohibited. No part of this book may be reproduced or transmitted in any form or by any means, electronic or mechanical, including photocopying, recording, or by any information storage and retrieval system without express written permission from the author/publisher.

I have tried to recreate events, locales and conversations from my memories of them. In order to maintain their anonymity in some instances, I have changed the names of individuals and places and I may have changed some identifying characteristics and details such as physical properties, occupations and places of residence.

Although the author and publisher have made every effort to ensure that the information in this book was correct at press time, the author and publisher do not assume and hereby disclaim any liability to any party for any loss, damage, or disruption caused by errors or omissions, whether such errors or omissions result from negligence, accident, or any other cause.

Note from the Author

Hey you! Thank you for purchasing the Book of Boundaries (Sapphire edition). Before you proceed any further into this book series, I want to share my heart with you regarding this series. After having ministered to or counseled countless women about boundary-setting, it became apparent that the issues that are ever-so-prevalent in this world are mainly centered around a need for boundaries. I can truly say that more than ninety percent of the people I've coached, counseled or mentored were in dire straits simply because they didn't have any solid or healthy boundaries set in their lives. In truth, most people have never had anyone to teach them how to properly set boundaries. Consequently, our mental institutions and prisons are overflowing with people whose minds have been taken over by the enemy. All the same, school shootings, racism, divorce, rape, abuse and essentially every evil thing on Earth has been thriving as the human race continues to descend into madness. This is why I created the Book of Boundaries!

You'll notice that there are five parts to this series. They are:
1. The Onyx Edition
2. The Emerald Edition
3. **The Sapphire Edition** (You are here)
4. The Jasper Edition
5. The Ruby Edition

I chose these names for several reasons, but mainly

because of their colors and what those colors represent. All the same, each of these stones could be found in the ephod of the high priest. "Ye have seen what I did unto the Egyptians, and how I bare you on eagles' wings, and brought you unto myself. Now therefore, if ye will obey my voice indeed, and keep my covenant, then ye shall be a peculiar treasure unto me above all people: for all the earth is mine: And ye shall be unto me a <u>kingdom of priests</u>, and an holy nation. These are the words which thou shalt speak unto the children of Israel" (Exodus 19:4-6). Believers are priests or priestesses of the Most High God, and as such, we should not be in bondage to any person or system that is contrary to our design! This means that these books are all about IDENTITY! They will help you to better understand who you are, and give you the confidence needed to embrace your God-given identity! Once you do this, it will be easier for you to appreciate yourself enough to establish boundaries.

Each of these books represent your exodus from one mindset to another one. You won't just learn about boundaries, but you will learn a lot about yourself while reading this series! You will learn about demonology, relationships and how the enemy advances against the minds of God's people by simply using the technology of ignorance! You will go from black to blue, from not knowing to understanding why it is necessary for you to set boundaries, what it looks and feels like to live behind boundaries, and what you stand to gain once you effectively set and enforce boundaries in your life. You will learn about the infamous narcissist and how to rid your life of that evil force once and for all. This is a must-have book for the sane and the insane! It is designed to help you to take back the real estate of your mind that the enemy has stolen from you!

In this series, I also shared some of my personal stories and dreams with you so that you can also witness the exodus that I had to take from being a mess to a living message! I shared these stories so that you can know that it is POSSIBLE for you to completely leave and annihilate one mindset and lifestyle, and wholeheartedly embrace another lifestyle that looks NOTHING like the one you left behind!

Welcome to the Book of Boundaries! Warning: revelation produces a paradigmatic shift, which causes things in your life that shouldn't be there to wither up and fall away. In other words, if you like being broken, bound and miserable, don't go any further because the revelation in this series is potent enough to sober you up! But if you're ready for a change, flip the page!

Sincerely,
Tiffany Buckner

Introduction

The Sapphire Edition

Scriptures for this Edition

Let us draw near with a true heart in full assurance of faith, having our hearts sprinkled from an evil conscience, and our bodies washed with pure water.
Hebrews 10:22

And he shewed me a pure river of water of life, clear as crystal, proceeding out of the throne of God and of the Lamb.
Revelation 22:1

He that believeth on me, as the scripture hath said, out of his belly shall flow rivers of living water.
John 7:38

The sapphire stone is BLUE.

The color blue, in this edition, represents purity; it represents the aftermath of God's refining power. The Hebrews crossed over the Red Sea, and the ones who did not rebel against God (some generations later) crossed over into the Promised Land, a territory that the Bible describes as flowing with milk and honey. This means abundance! Whenever there is purity, abundance is inevitable. Think back to the book of Genesis when God purified the waters and then, filled them with life. This not only means that you will live again, but the promises of God in your life that have been spoken over your family generations ago will come to pass!

This edition is all about breakthrough! The Sapphire edition was written to bring you clarity. It brings together the information that you took from the first two editions and marries that information together to produce a revelation so potent that it will change the way you see life! Also note that the color blue represents purification; this is because fire, when it is this color, is at its hottest, ranging between 2,600° Fahrenheit and 3,000° Fahrenheit!

Table of Contents

Note from the Author..III
Introduction...VII
Spiritual Boundaries...1
Sexual Boundaries..37
Financial Boundaries...93
Heart Boundaries...121
Your Neighborhood of Thinking...163
    Blame Culture and Entitlement......................................167
    Victimhood...183
Understanding Rejection..199
    Transitioning..220
    Resisting Temptation..222
The Shape of a Season..233
Move On..251
A Note to the Empath and the Prophetic Individual...........267

SPIRITUAL BOUNDARIES

The date was March 24th, 2020. The sound of my alarm pierced the darkness, scaring me out of my sleep and ripping me out of the pages of a nightmare. Now, I'm not an avid dreamer. I do dream from time to time, and there are some seasons when I dream a lot, but for the most part, I'm not a person who has dreams every night (that I can remember, at least). Howbeit, whenever I do have a dream, it is often very detailed and meaningful. Either that or I pay close attention to the details.

I dreamed that I was back in Mississippi and I was living in an old house of mine, but here's the weird part—the outside of the house looked like a house I shared with my ex-husband, but the inside of the house looked like the house I'd lived in when I was around eight-years old. And somehow, I identified the house as my house, but my mother had a room in the house, so it almost felt like it was her house too—if that makes sense. My mother said to me that she was about to go somewhere and she'd be back. Also, she was taking my little sister with her. I'm not sure where she was supposed to be headed to. And honestly, I don't remember seeing her in the dream. I think she may have called. I just remember hearing her voice and knowing that she'd stepped out.

In the dream, I came across an ex of mine. Now, mind you,

the ex in my dream wasn't the ex-husband I'd shared the actual house with; he was someone I'd briefly dated when I was around twenty-years old. He was an older guy; maybe ten or fifteen years my senior. In the dream, we talked, and somehow, I let him come into my house, even though I wasn't sure about reconciling with him. Almost immediately, I felt a sense of regret. I wanted him to get out of my house, so I asked him to leave, but he refused. He became aggressive and emotional, and it was clear to me that I was going to have to have him removed from my house. I couldn't call the cops because he monitored my every movement, so I came up with a plan to get rid of him. I knew that if I got him to come outside of the house, he wouldn't be able to get back in because he didn't have a key. So, I told him that I needed to go to the store and I asked him if he wanted to go to the store with me. He agreed.

Now, here's where it gets interesting. On the way to the store, I noticed that we were in another one of my childhood neighborhoods, and not the same neighborhood that the house was in that I'd shared with my ex-husband, neither was it the same neighborhood as the house I'd lived in at eight-years old (we moved at least once a year up until I was around eleven-years old). We were in the neighborhood that I'd lived in from the ages of 11 to 13, and I was walking towards the store. So, picture this—I was pretty much in three places at one time.

1. The outside of the house looked like the house I'd shared with my first ex-husband.

2. The inside of the house looked like a house I'd lived in when I was eight-years old.
3. The neighborhood looked like the neighborhood I'd lived in when I was 11-years old.

So, the dream took place in three realms. Again, asking him to go to the store with me was my way of getting the ex out of my house; I wanted him out of my life once and for all. But what's even more interesting is, we were walking on one street divided into two parts; it was almost like it was two streets, but it had been separated by a large amount of space. Both roads were narrow. The best way that I can describe it is—it appeared to be a street that had been perfectly split in half during an earthquake or some type of natural disaster. Between the streets was what appeared to be a large pit or gulf that separated both the streets from one another. I was on one side of the street and the ex was on the other side, but we were walking in the same direction. I'm pretty sure that had I went to look at the space that separated both streets, I would have seen a bottomless pit. In other words, there was no way for him to get to me and there was no way for me to get to him. Nevertheless, I identified it as the same street; it was almost like a mirror of two dimensions!

The ex had three small children following up behind him, but he wasn't paying them any attention. They were playing, all the while, trying to keep up with him, but he was focused on me. I don't remember what he was saying. I just remember responding a few times. But I started realizing more and more that he couldn't get to me because we were on the same street in two different dimensions. Again, the street was divided by what appeared to be a deep pit, so I decided to use that opportunity to run. I suddenly switched directions and started running towards what appeared to be a small store (not the same store I had been walking towards). I could hear my ex screaming out my name while crying, and I somehow knew that he was trying to pursue me, but I didn't care. I passionately wanted him out of my house and my life once and for all.

I arrived at a small mom and pop's store and found two older men standing outside. They reminded me of some of the older fatherly type guys you'd see kinda lounging around a mom and pop's structure in the South. They were just standing there talking to each other when I approached them. I told the men what had happened and asked one of the men to call the cops. He agreed to do so and went into the building to make the call. I then told the other guy my dilemma. He was compassionate and understanding. I don't remember the advice he gave me, but I do remember him advising me. He was very fatherly and I felt safe in his presence. I felt at peace in his presence. "The cops are on the way," the other guy said as he came out the door. Somehow, I knew that he meant the cops would meet me at my house, so I thanked the men and went home.

At home, I called a former friend of mine. In the dream, she and I were still friends. Just to give you a little history, I was friends with this young lady for more than twenty years. Our friendship didn't necessarily end on bad terms; we just transitioned out of the friendship. In short, we just stopped calling each other. But in the dream, we were still close friends. I called her and told her about my dilemma. Just like she'd done in the past, she told me to come over to her house until my mother came back. I agreed, but I told her that I was waiting on the cops so I could file a report. That's when my doorbell rang. "Hold on," I said as I walked towards the door, convinced that it was someone from the police department. "I think the police are outside." But when I opened the front door, I was greeted by an unfamiliar face. The guy standing before me was a postal worker or a UPS agent; either way, he was there to deliver a package to me. The package was a large opened box, and inside the box, I saw countless bottles of motor oil. I looked at the delivery guy and said, "I didn't order that." That's when I heard my ex's voice. "I ordered it," he said. When I looked to my right, I saw my ex sitting down on my porch almost out of view. He had gotten a fresh haircut and he was dressed to impress. "You can't ship anything here!" I shouted. "You don't live here anymore!" He became very agitated and began to shout over me, "I do live here!" This shouting match continued until the delivery guy disappeared into thin air. The delivery guy wasn't able to deliver the package because I had refused it, and my ex couldn't come back in because he didn't have my permission to do so, nor did he have a key.

Again, as quickly as he'd appeared, the delivery guy seemed to disappear. I went back in, closed the door and started telling my former friend about the event. That's when my doorbell rang again. "Stay on the phone with me," she said. "Just in case it's him." I was sure it was, but I didn't want to miss the cops, so I opened the door. That's when I saw two female cops. With my ex still sitting on my porch, I told the officers about my dilemma. It was clear to me that they couldn't do anything but reiterate to him that he couldn't come back in my house, even though he kept screaming, "I'm not leaving! This is my house!" He was inconsolable, and if you didn't know any better, you'd almost feel sorry for the guy. He was like a broken man fighting with all of his might for his failed relationship. So, I asked one of the officers if she'd wait for me. I said, "Ma'am, I don't feel comfortable staying here, knowing that he's on the loose. Can you wait outside until I get my things? I'm going to go stay at my friend's house." The officer was very nice and accommodating. "I just need five minutes," I said. It was clear to me that the officer wished she could do more. She had so much love and compassion in her eyes that it was almost overwhelming. "Sure," she said. "I'll wait more than five minutes if you need me to." Her voice was so loving and calming that it helped to relax me. I thanked her and then, closed the door. That's when I went into my mother's room to collect a few things. I don't remember what I found on her bed (I'm pretty sure it was a used, balled up tissue); I just remember that it was out of place, so I picked it up because I didn't want to leave the room in disarray. I also remember thinking that I needed to call her to let her know what was going on. After that, the alarm went off and scared me out of my sleep.

The dream had so many layers to it. Thankfully, God has given me the gift of dream interpretation, but this hasn't been a gift that I've shared with the world because it's still in development. (Additionally, when people realize that you have that gift, you'll get a ton of calls, emails and instant messages from people on a daily basis wanting you to interpret their dreams.) All the same, God doesn't give me the interpretation of everybody's dreams. A brother in Christ asked me to interpret a dream for him, and I was stumped. I prayed for the revelation, but I got nothing. So, God clearly withholds some revelation for a specific time or He shares it through specific people at specific times. But again, the dream had many layers to it. First off, the man in the dream represented a familiar spirit. Whenever you dream about familiar faces, especially if the dream is dark or demonic, the person doesn't necessarily represent the individual you see in the dream. He or she represents a familiar spirit. This is important to note because more than fifty percent of Christians misinterpret their dreams whenever they see familiar faces. For example, if a woman dreams about her ex and she dreams that they reconciled, she'd likely wake up thinking that God was showing her snippets of her future. She'd be convinced that she and her ex were going to get back together, and that's not necessarily what that dream meant. Consequently, she'd spend more time soul-tied to her ex, instead of getting the healing, help, understanding and deliverance she needs to move forward. But let's look at the layers and the interpretations God gave me. Note: I'm sure that there is more revelation that will come to me over the next few days, months and years.

I was back in Mississippi: I was born and raised in Mississippi, and to be honest with you, I'd had a very traumatic childhood. For this reason, I left the state more than a decade ago and I hadn't looked back. In all truth, I hadn't planned to ever look back; that is, until my mother was fighting for her life. I hadn't been to Mississippi for nine or ten years before I drove down there to pick up my ailing mother. Two or three years before that happened, I'd gone through deliverance. I used to fly my mother to Georgia, and eventually, the Cancer Treatment Centers of America started flying her here. While she was here, I'd arranged for her to receive the ministry of deliverance. After the man of God prayed for her (over video), he asked to speak with me. When I got on the line, he asked me if he could pray for me. He then told me that I'd been so traumatized in my childhood that those spirits had me afraid to return to the state of Mississippi. Honestly, I'd never associated my refusal to reenter the state with me being fearful of it, nevertheless, the minute he said that, fear manifested and I began to weep uncontrollably. So, me being back in Mississippi in the dream represented an old state of mind I'd had. It represented my past.

The outside of the house looked like the house I'd shared with my ex, the inside looked like a house I'd lived in at the age of eight, and the neighborhood looked like a neighborhood I'd lived in between the ages of 11-13. This represented different markers in my past. In each of these places, I'd undergone some of the most traumatic events of my life. Amazingly enough, out of all the places we lived when I was a child, I remember those places the most because of those experiences. Additionally, I'd lived in three houses with my ex over the course of our marriage, but the house I'd dreamed of was the one where I'd endured the most abuse. These markers likely detailed the points and places in which that familiar spirit had entered my life or done the most damage in my life. All the same, I am the house. Anytime you dream about a house, the structure represents you (body and soul).

He was an ex and I let him into my house, knowing that he wanted to move in with me. Howbeit, the same day he'd come in is the day I'd asked him to leave. I was pretty much flirting with the idea of reconciliation, but I quickly decided against it; besides, there was "no room" for him in my place because my mother and sister were living there. This part of the dream is clearly detailing what the Bible deems as the return of the unclean spirit. "When the unclean spirit is gone out of a man, he walketh through dry places, seeking rest, and findeth none. Then he saith, I will return into <u>my house</u> from whence I came out; and when he is come, <u>he findeth it empty, swept, and garnished</u>. Then goeth he, and taketh with himself seven other spirits more wicked than himself, and they enter in and dwell there: and the last state of that man is worse than the first. Even so shall it be also unto this wicked generation" (Matthew 12:43-45). Notice that I underlined the part where the scripture says, "He finds it empty, swept and garnished." My house had been filled; it was no longer empty, and because I saw it as my house and my mother's house as well, I didn't have the legal right to let that guy stay there. I would have needed my mother's permission. Now, mind you, in this dream, my mother was a representation of Christ Jesus. God is the Father, so in this scenario, Jesus represents the Mother. In John 14:3, Jesus said, "And if I go and prepare a place for you, I will come again, and receive you unto myself; that where I am, there ye may be also." This is why my mother was gone in the dream. As for my sister, I believe that my actual mother was my sister in the dream. My mother passed away in October of 2018.

It became clear to me that I was going to have to get help removing him from my house. This represents deliverance, but deliverance is more than a "come up and come out" command. It's taking a legal stance against something. In the dream, I called the cops. They are officers of the law. They come to enforce the laws and the statutes of any given jurisdiction. So, the help wasn't necessarily another person; it meant that I had to deal with the issue legally. Remember what Jesus said to the disciples after they were unable to cast out a spirit that had been tormenting a young boy. The boy's father had come to them seeking help, but the disciples couldn't help him. In his frustration, the father had turned to Jesus for help. Jesus rebuked the disciples, and when they'd asked Him why they were unable to cast out the unclean spirit, He replied, "This kind can come forth by nothing, but by prayer and fasting." Some spirits are not cast out in a traditional deliverance setting; they are evicted after the person goes before the King of kings and the Lord of lords in fasting and prayer. They come out when the person approaches the Courts of Heaven! Thankfully, this particular spirit was an "ex." He'd already been removed, but to permanently remove him, I had to fast him out, not cast him out.

I asked him to walk with me to the store. Amazingly enough, the street I was on led to an old store that I used to frequent when I was young, but of course, the store represented the "storehouse." This represented the church. The store I had been heading towards was a large store, but when I switched directions, I went to a small store. I'll explain the significance of this shortly.

He had three children running behind him. Those children represented other demonic spirits. He was the strongman; they were the henchmen. They were children because of their rank. Most deliverance ministers call them "imps." Now understand that there is no such thing as a baby demon; they are all timeless. They are all ancient forces, so whenever you see a small child in a dream and that child happens to be evil, the child represents a low-ranking spirit—possibly a spirit you've defeated and could easily and effortlessly defeat again. Also, remember that a spirit that ranks low to you may be a high-ranking spirit to someone else.

We were on two separate roads, heading in the same direction. This is a legality. He had no legal access to me anymore. Once I got him out of my house, he lost access to me. We were no longer in agreement, so he couldn't walk with me. Amos 3:3 states, "Can two walk together, except they be agreed?" The fact that we were heading in the same direction isn't alarming; it simply meant that he was pursuing me. The divide between us represents a boundary; it is a gulf that cannot be crossed. This reminds me of the story of the rich man who went to hell. Luke 16:19-31 reads, "There was a certain rich man, which was clothed in purple and fine linen, and fared sumptuously every day: And there was a certain beggar named Lazarus, which was laid at his gate, full of sores, and desiring to be fed with the crumbs which fell from the rich man's table: moreover the dogs came and licked his sores. And it came to pass, that the beggar died, and was carried by the angels into Abraham's bosom: the rich man also died, and was buried; And in hell he lift up his eyes, being in torments, and seeth Abraham afar off, and Lazarus in his bosom. And he cried and said, Father Abraham, have mercy on me, and send Lazarus, that he may dip the tip of his finger in water, and cool my tongue; for I am tormented in this flame. But Abraham said, Son, remember that thou in thy lifetime receivedst thy good things, and likewise Lazarus evil things: but now he is comforted, and thou art tormented. And beside all this, between us and you there is a <u>great gulf fixed</u>: so that they which would pass from hence to you cannot; neither can they pass to us, that would come from thence. Then he said, I pray thee therefore, father, that thou wouldest send him to my father's house: For I have five brethren; that he may testify unto them, lest they also come into this place of torment. Abraham saith unto him, They have Moses and the prophets; let them hear them. And he said, Nay, father Abraham: but if one went unto them from the dead, they will repent. And he said unto him, If they hear not Moses and the prophets, neither will they be persuaded, though one rose from the dead."

Notice in this parable, there is a mention of a fixed gulf. This is a boundary, and this boundary represents a legality. This means that he couldn't legally cross over to where I was, and I couldn't legally cross over to where he was. This hadn't been the first time I'd dreamed about something separating me from a spirit disguised as a person. At the age of ten, I'd had a series of dreams, and in those dreams, I was standing on one side of a fence, and some young boy around my age was standing on the other side of the fence. The fence reached all the way up to Heaven; you couldn't see where it started or where it ended, both horizontally and vertically. The boy couldn't speak. I remember him being fair-skinned with a face full of freckles. Being a child, I didn't know that the dream was demonic. At that stage, I didn't even know what a demon was! Nevertheless, I had this dream maybe three or more times, and in each instance, we were staring at each other through the fence. He didn't look menacing; he looked loving and sad that the fence kept us separate. He would grip the fence and walk whenever I walked. That was the fullness of that dream. Was it the same spirit I was now dreaming about? Possibly! He was small in that dream, not because I'd defeated him (because I hadn't), but because I was young. In other words, he had to match my rank! "So shall they fear the name of the LORD from the west, and his glory from the rising of the sun. When the enemy shall come in like a flood, the Spirit of the LORD shall lift up a standard against him" (Isaiah 59:19). A standard is a measure of rule; it is a limitation or a boundary. In that dream, the fence represented a standard; it represented a boundary that the Lord had given the enemy! It was a hedge of protection; it was a guard rail!

I suddenly switched directions and started running towards a small store. This is a historic event; it is a marker from my past! It is the moment I switched directions or, better yet, repented! To repent means to turn around or to switch directions. And this is truly how it had happened! My salvation had been suddenly. I was driving home from the club one night with a friend in my car. We were both drunk and we'd almost had an accident. That's when she suggested that we get our lives together and start going to church. That next Sunday, we went to church, and three

Sundays later, I approached the altar for salvation. The building that I ran towards in the dream isn't just the church, but I ran towards Christ. My family was religious, but unrepentant. They went to church out of religious obligation whenever they did go. So, when I told the "ex" I was going to church, that spirit thought I was heading towards religion. This was the "big store" I had been heading towards. Instead, I switched directions (generationally) and ran toward an intimate relationship with God.

I arrived at the building and found two older men standing outside. Again, they felt like father-figures. One went inside to call the cops for me; the other stayed outside with me. He was relaxed and there wasn't an ounce of fear on his face. For this reason, I felt safe in his presence. Of course, he represents Father God! I'd run to God (in prayer), and He sent help my way in the form of the Holy Spirit!

After they called the cops, I thanked the men and went home. "Home" in this sense doesn't represent a physical structure; it denotes my identity. I came to myself. In short, I began to realize who I am in Christ Jesus, so I stopped running from my past and decided to walk in my God-given authority. The enemy had successfully stolen my identity generations ago by stealing my family's identity. We didn't know who we were; this is why we'd moved around a lot when I was young. All of the moving and shuffling had been the result of my parents' financial struggles. Thankfully, they'd always managed to stay above water, but they were always making adjustments in their attempts to stay afloat in their sea of debt. Anytime an individual has substantial financial disparities, that individual has an identity issue. Our success is tied to our identities.

I called a former friend of mine. In the dream, she was still a close friend. This represents prayer. I called on the name of the Lord and He set me free. "No longer do I call you servants, for the servant does not know what his master is doing; but I have called you friends, for all that I have heard from my Father I have made known to you" (John 15:15). All the same, she told me to come over to her house until my mother came back. Translated, God invited me into His perfect peace. Amazingly enough, I used to run to this old friend's house anytime my ex and I would get into a fight. She used to always urge me to come over to her house before things got out of control, but I rarely listened, reasoning within myself that I could keep the matter from escalating. She'd lost her mother to domestic violence, so she'd passionately tried to get me to get out of that marriage, but I was young and foolish. I thought I had everything under control. When I finally did get out, she opened her home to me again, urging me not to go back to my mother's house. My mother had a live-in boyfriend at that time who made me (and every female who visited my mother's house) extremely uncomfortable. So, I'd lived with her for a month or so before returning to my mother's house.

The doorbell rang. When I opened the door, I was

greeted by a postal worker or some type of delivery guy trying to deliver motor oil. He was a demonic agent. What's remarkable is the fact that my ex was outside, but he didn't have a key (legal access) to reenter my home, so he used a demonic agent in his attempt to gain entry. The motor oil represents dark oil. The anointing oil of God is pure, but this agent was trying to use dark oil (witchcraft) to regain entry. Needless to say, it didn't work. Amazingly enough, the box contained a lot of motor oil. All the same, the box was open, meaning, there was nothing hidden from me. God allowed me to clearly see the enemy's next vice.

He had gotten a fresh haircut and he was dressed to impress. Apostle Paul described this dilemma in 1 Corinthians 11:14. He said, "And no marvel; for Satan himself is transformed into an angel of light." In short, he was trying to appeal to my natural senses; this deals with sensuality. He was trying to look harmless when, in truth, he was a devil!

We argued about him living there. He was inconsolable. This is normal demonic behavior. When a demon loses its house or place of residence, it is terrified. But when it said "house," it wasn't referencing the structure I was in; it was referencing me. That's why that spirit followed me to the "store." It didn't want the building; it wanted me. Once I refused the oil, the delivery guy disappeared and two female officers showed up. This reminds me of the moment Jesus was tempted in the wilderness by Satan. After He'd passed the tests, the Bible says that angels came and ministered to Him.

Two female cops showed up; one was really patient and kind. The other wasn't mean. I just don't remember talking with her. The first cop represented the Holy Spirit. The other cop was an angel of God. Of course, they were patient and kind because God's angels exude His character. They stood outside the house, guarding it and disallowing the ex to reenter while I was inside getting ready to leave.

I closed the door and went into my mother's room to collect somethings. In this part of the dream, my mother no longer represented Christ; her room represented a generational issue. I found something out of place on her bed, so I picked it up. What was I doing? Cleaning up the room; I was cleaning up my bloodline! Why was it on the bed? The bed is a place of intimacy; it pretty much told me what type of spirit I had been dealing with. It was a spirit of lust and perversion, and again, it got cast out a long time ago, but the dream signified its attempt to return. It couldn't, because I'd cleaned up the room (bloodline), and I'd allowed God to fill that space.

At this point, the alarm went off and I sat up on my bed. Believe it or not, the dream encompassed both the past and my present. And more than that, it dealt with boundaries. I'd once allowed the enemy in my life because I lacked knowledge, but the more I got to know YAHWEH, the more I began to fill my temple with His Word. I studied, I prayed and I repented. I submitted, I confessed my sins and I grew. Eventually, the woman I was died to herself, and a new creature (in Christ Jesus) appeared. I divorced the devil. I divorced his lies, I divorced his doctrines and I divorced his plans for me. I kept doing this until James 4:7 took full effect—"Submit yourselves therefore to God. Resist the devil, and he will flee from you." My deliverance hadn't taken place at a church altar; it had taken place over the course of time at the altar of decision! I'd decided to forgive my adversaries, I'd decided to turn away from fornication, I'd decided to love myself, and then I learned to love others the way I love myself. I came to understand that the most effective deliverance takes place when we change our minds! I'd studied the Word and allowed God to transform my mind until perversion could find no place left in me!

Spiritual boundaries are just that—boundaries placed in the realm of the spirit. In the book of Job, Satan said to God that He had placed a hedge of protection around Job. He asked God to lift the hedge. Of course, the hedge represents a boundary. It is a line of demarcation or a standard. Isaiah 59:19 states, "So shall they fear the name of the LORD from the west, and His glory from the rising of the sun; when the enemy comes in like a flood, the Spirit of the LORD will lift up a standard against him." What is a standard? The Greek word is "kanón," and according to Strong's Concordance, it means "a rule, regulation, rule of conduct or doctrine." What rule of conduct did God lift against Satan in Job's case? He allowed Satan to attack and test Job, but He also drew a line in the sand. "And the LORD said to Satan, 'Behold, he is in your hand; only spare his life.'" He lifted the boundary and allowed Satan to attack Job on every side, but the one thing that Satan could not take was Job's life. This is reminiscent of the series of dreams I'd had at the age of ten when I'd dreamed of the little boy staring at me from the other side of a long and tall fence. That little boy was the devil! Now imagine what would have happened had God removed that fence! The hell I'd gone through was child's play in comparison to what I would have suffered had God removed His hedge of protection from around me.

Believe it or not, God has fences around His children. We may feel overwhelmed at times, and it may feel like the storms we find ourselves in are too much for us, but in truth, they are not. Every storm is an opportunity for us to tap into the dominion and authority that God has afforded us through His Son, Christ Yeshua. For example, whenever you find yourself under demonic attack, your assignment is to get from under it; your assignment is to bring it under you, but to do this, you have to first remember that you are a spirit living in a body. You have to know your God-given identity! Why is this important? Because most believers identify themselves by what they see in the mirror. Consequently, they spend more time decorating the outer man (body) than they do preparing the inner man (spirit). So, when they go under a spiritual attack, they try to fight back with their flesh. For example, let's say that a woman at your job has been spreading gossip and lies about you. You don't personally know her, so you don't know or understand why she's investing her time and energy into destroying your reputation. Chances are, the fight isn't natural; it's spiritual. You see, the woman in question may be bound, for example, by a spirit of deep hurt. Some woman may have been a willing participant in the destruction of her last relationship, and you may remind her of that woman. Because she's never forgiven the woman or healed from the relationship, she may be attacking you simply because you look like the other woman. Then again, you may remind her of her abusive mother. This isn't fair; it's silly, foolish and petty, but it does happen. If you're not careful, you'll focus on her flesh and not what's operating behind the scenes of that vessel. When this happens, you become spiritually impotent in that particular battle simply because you're focusing on the vessel that's attacking you, and not the captain behind the "will" of that vessel. I like to say it this way—every puppet has a master. When I learned this truth, I stopped focusing on the puppet and I started focusing on the one pulling the strings. When you focus on the person and what you perceive to be that person's agenda, it's easy for you to get involved in either low-level or high-level witchcraft. This is why you have to attack it in the spirit through prayer, fasting and by loving the unlovable.

Every attack has a purpose behind it. The sad part is, the average Christian focuses on the surface of the issue; this is what's apparent, but a lot of what we endure is spiritual, even though we can clearly see the skin and teeth of the people who Satan uses to attack, persecute and demean us. This is just a distraction. This is also why Ephesians 6:12 says, "For we wrestle not against flesh and blood, but against principalities, against powers, against the rulers of the darkness of this world, against spiritual wickedness in high places." I can think of several instances where I became distracted by the exterior (the assailant) and not the spirit behind the matter. This is why it is good to have mentors. I can also think of a few times when a mentor steered me in the right direction, especially when I was a babe in Christ. One of my mentors would often point out to me that I was being distracted by what I saw, and I wasn't paying attention to the spirit behind the matter. Before I'd met him, I was constantly finding myself in the snares of unforgiveness. This was because I had trouble forgiving people who disliked and persecuted me for no obvious reason, especially if I'd gone out of my way to get along with those people. I'd eventually forgive them and move on, but this was a snare I constantly found myself in. God started sending me mentors when I didn't have a church home. Needless to say, Satan sent a couple of them as well! That particular mentor taught me the basics of demonology. He helped me through some of the roughest patches in my early Christian walk. Another guy who mentored me was an older man in his early seventies. He'd reached out to me in the year 2009 and said to me, "I don't know who you are! I don't know anything about you! All I know is that God wants me to mentor you in spiritual warfare! If you agree to this, give me a call!" After this, he listed his number. Now, mind you, I was in one of the biggest spiritual fights of my life at that time and only the people closest to me knew this. I hadn't posted about it to social media.

At that time, I didn't understand spiritual boundaries. I'd just learned about demons a year prior to that. I'd gotten remarried in 2008, and in 2009, my ex and I traveled to one of his relatives' houses. Without going too far into detail, I found myself in this woman's house, holding a coffee cup. Inside that coffee cup was olive oil that I'd just had a friend of mine to help me bless. Again, I didn't understand spiritual boundaries, but when I look back, I can see how I also violated some very practical boundaries as well. In other words, I invited a lot of the chaos and attacks that I found myself enduring. The woman despised me because she'd tried to indoctrinate me into their beliefs, but I wouldn't budge. I was a babe in Christ, and it had just become clear to me that I hadn't asked the right questions while courting the man. All the same, he hadn't been entirely honest with me about his beliefs; he'd led me to believe that, while his family believed in and practiced ancestral worship, he did not. Nevertheless, this relative of his was overly determined to convert me, not just in my spiritual and religious beliefs, but also about life. Her views were obviously demonic, and they'd been skewed by pain, trauma, anger and, of course, false doctrine. The woman was into ancestral worship and a host of other ungodly practices, and I'd angered her because I had refused to accept her views as my own despite her passionate attempts to get me to see things her way. After she couldn't convert me, she tried to intimidate me into changing my mind, saying things like, "The wife is supposed to follow the husband," and "In my country, you don't just marry the man, you marry his family, so I am also your husband! That means that you have to listen to me and do as I say!" I refused. I didn't do it. I couldn't do it. I just could not go under her headship or accept her views. It just wasn't in me. I'm being honest when I say that it almost felt impossible for me to take direction from her. Every time she tried to lead me astray, a fire would rise up in me and I'd find myself passionately talking about Christ Jesus. After that, she stopped speaking to me, so my entire stay in her house became very awkward and uncomfortable. She began trying to sabotage me in every way, even telling me not to eat any of the food in her house and telling me that she was going to "take" her relative back from me. My ex and I had never argued so much in our lives with one another, but anytime we went to her house, we did not and could not get along at all. So, one day, I found myself holding a cup of oil that I'd blessed, ready to cross another boundary. My ex wasn't there and neither was his relative, so I went throughout the house drawing crosses on the doors with the oil and pleading the blood of Jesus. Oh, how wrong I was! First off, on a practical or personal level, this is disrespectful. You should NEVER attempt to bless someone's house without that person's permission, but I didn't know this at the time. I made the crosses faint so no one could see them, but the enemy saw them! I did this maybe two or three times, and every time I blessed the house, there would be peace in that place for an entire day, but the next day, all hell would break loose! I'd unknowingly crossed a boundary, and after telling my first mentor what I'd done, I'd gotten the rebuke of a lifetime. He said to me (paraphrased), "Tiffany, you can't go into the devil's house and rebuke him! She's dedicated her house to the devil! That's his house! That's why you keep going through so much warfare!" In other words, I'd crossed a boundary or two. He told me that the moment I realized she was into witchcraft, I should have left and gotten a hotel room. I should have refused to stay there. He was right. I just didn't know any better at that stage of my development, and this is why I emphasize the importance of mentors. The older gentleman reached out to me around that time as well, and he pretty much gave me the same advice. Unlike my first mentor, the older gentleman had once pastored a church, but he'd retired from pastoring. He was familiar with demonology and the ministry of deliverance, so he taught me, for example, how to pray warfare prayers. He also taught me about spiritual boundaries. I believe he was the first person who told me that I was called to the ministry of deliverance. Both of these men were pivotal in my early development.

Spiritual boundaries go both ways. For example, in the dream I'd had, the "ex" was on the same road I was on in another dimension. He couldn't cross the gulf that separated us, and I couldn't cross it either. Now, this didn't mean that it was entirely impossible for us to at least attempt to cross those gulfs; this simply means that it was and is illegal for us to cross those gulfs. There was a deep pit separating both dimensions; this was the gulf. Howbeit, Christians attempt to cross these gulfs all the time. This is how they end up bound; this is how they end up in ditches. Another word for "ditch" is "pit." A pit is a deep, dark hole that was often used as a dungeon. This is why, in the ministry of deliverance, you'll hear the deliverance workers telling a demonic spirit to go to the abyss or into the pit. Very few ministers use the phrase "bottomless pit," but it is still used. The word "bottomless" isn't necessarily dealing with the absence of land; it's not referencing a vertical space to which there is no end. It pretty much means timeless or eternal. If you'll notice, the word "eternal" cannot be measured by time, nor does it fit within the realm or concept of time because it is not an earthly concept. Even this world will come to an end, so eternity is a supernatural concept that cannot fit into natural logic. It simply means never-ending. Again, spiritual boundaries are two-sided. For example, a Christian reading his or her horoscope has already attempted to cross this gulf. Christians who practice necromancy have already attempted to cross this gulf. Christians who engage in any type of spiritual practice without the leading or guidance of the Holy Spirit have already attempted to cross this gulf. This is how they ended up bound. This is how their children end up being the subject of generational curses. Think of it this way—you're falling, and you've been falling for several years. You've never reached the bottom (conclusion) of whatever it is you've fallen into. While on the way down, you give birth to three children. What do you imagine that they would be doing? Falling, of course! This is why the Bible says that if the blind leads the blind, they will both fall into a ditch! This is all because someone attempted to cross a boundary that they were never supposed to cross. Remember, any time you cross a boundary, you'll end up bound.

In my dream, the "ex" could not come into my house unless I invited him there. Once I kicked him out, he could not come back in without a key. Notice, he was in the dream, sitting on my porch, just a few feet away from two officers. They didn't arrest him; they didn't bind him. They simply warned him. Had he tried to force himself into the house, he would have been easily bound. Demons know their limits, and while they hate boundaries, they have to respect them. This is why they try to drive people into sin because the place of faithlessness (sin) is their legal domain.

And finally, there are spiritual boundaries in the ministry of deliverance. If I were to stand in a room filled with men and women and say, "There are some demons you can't cast out because they outrank you," someone would either raise their hand and blurt out Luke 10:19, which reads, "Behold, I give unto you power to tread on serpents and scorpions, and over all the power of the enemy: and nothing shall by any means hurt you." They'd then argue that Jesus gave us authority over all the power of the enemy, and they would be right in Word, but they'd be lacking in understanding. You can quote

Spiritual Boundaries

a scripture and speak truth, all the while, not understand what you're saying. As Christians, we do have authority over the enemy and all of his power, but even the angels recognize rank! Let's look at two instances to better understand how rank works!

Situation Number One

Daniel 10:10-14: And, behold, an hand touched me, which set me upon my knees and upon the palms of my hands. And he said unto me, O Daniel, a man greatly beloved, understand the words that I speak unto thee, and stand upright: for unto thee am I now sent. And when he had spoken this word unto me, I stood trembling. Then said he unto me, Fear not, Daniel: for from the first day that thou didst set thine heart to understand, and to chasten thyself before thy God, thy words were heard, and I am come for thy words. But the prince of the kingdom of Persia withstood me one and twenty days: but, lo, Michael, one of the chief princes, came to help me; and I remained there with the kings of Persia. Now I am come to make thee understand what shall befall thy people in the latter days: for yet the vision is for many days.

In this scripture, an angel of the Lord is talking to the prophet Daniel. He starts off describing why it took 21 days for Daniel's prayer to be answered. According to the angel, he'd come for Daniel's words, meaning, he had been sent to bring the answer to Daniel's prayers. However, the prince of Persia had come against or withstood this angel. In other words, the principality over Persia outranked this angel! If this wasn't true, the angel would not have needed other angelic assistance. So, Michael, who the Bible says is one of the chief princes, came and helped the angel. Angels come in ranks! There are archangels, which are high-ranking angels, just as there are angels. There are seraphim, cherubim and guardian angels. And no, your guardian angels are not your deceased loved ones! This isn't an exhaustive list, but the point I'm trying to make is that there are varying types of angels just as there are varying ranks of angels. All the same, there are varying types of demons just as there are varying ranks of demons. This is why, once again, when I'd dreamed about the "ex," he had three small children behind him. They were simply low-ranking spirits. They were a part of his demonic network.

But, someone will come along and say that this was "before" the death and resurrection of Jesus Christ! And now that Jesus has come and died for our sins, we no longer have to fast, pray and wait for a miracle to manifest. First and foremost, please understand that angels are timeless; they are not earthly vessels. They step into time when they are sent here, but they are from eternity; they are not subject to the dispensation of time. In eternity, no one ages because there is no death (as we know it); there is no time. Demons, on the other hand, were cast into the Earth; they are eternal creatures that are now being subjected to time! In other words, they will live forever, just like you and I will live forever because we are spirits locked inside of bodies.

Howbeit, they will be cast into hell; this is called the second death! Let's look at Matthew 8:28-29, which reads, "And when he was come to the other side into the country of the Gergesenes, there met him two possessed with devils, coming out of the tombs, exceeding fierce, so that no man might pass by that way. And, behold, they cried out, saying, What have we to do with thee, Jesus, thou Son of God? Art thou come hither to torment us before the time?" In this, the unclean spirits used the word "time." This means that they understood and still do understand that their day of reckoning will come; they are subject to time.

Our bodies are time capsules that allow us to live in the realm of the Earth, but once we leave these bodies, our spirit man doesn't sleep. Instead, we are instantly brought into the presence of God! This is why the Bible says that to be absent from the body is to be present with the Lord. So, in short, while we have authority over Satan and all of his angels, we still have to recognize rank. This brings us to the next instance.

Situation Number Two

Mark 9:16-29: And he asked the scribes, What question ye with them? And one of the multitude answered and said, Master, I have brought unto thee my son, which hath a dumb spirit; and wheresoever he taketh him, he teareth him: and he foameth, and gnasheth with his teeth, and pineth away: and I spake to thy disciples that they should cast him out; and they could not. He answereth him, and saith, O faithless

Spiritual Boundaries

generation, how long shall I be with you? How long shall I suffer you? Bring him unto me. And they brought him unto him: and when he saw him, straightway the spirit tare him; and he fell on the ground, and wallowed foaming. And he asked his father, How long is it ago since this came unto him? And he said, Of a child. And ofttimes it hath cast him into the fire, and into the waters, to destroy him: but if thou canst do any thing, have compassion on us, and help us. Jesus said unto him, If thou canst believe, all things are possible to him that believeth. And straightway the father of the child cried out, and said with tears, Lord, I believe; help thou mine unbelief. When Jesus saw that the people came running together, he rebuked the foul spirit, saying unto him, Thou dumb and deaf spirit, I charge thee, come out of him, and enter no more into him. And the spirit cried, and rent him sore, and came out of him: and he was as one dead; insomuch that many said, He is dead. But Jesus took him by the hand, and lifted him up; and he arose. And when he was come into the house, his disciples asked him privately, Why could not we cast him out? And he said unto them, This kind can come forth by nothing, but by prayer and fasting.

Now, in this scripture, we meet a desperate father who has a lunatic son. His son has been possessed by a demonic entity, and the father doesn't know what to do. So, he brought his son to Jesus' disciples, and they unsuccessfully attempted to administer deliverance to the young boy. So, the father brought his son to Jesus and told Him about his dilemma. Jesus cast the devil out of the child. After it was all said and done, the disciples waited for the crowd to dispense. When Jesus was alone with them, they asked Him, "Why couldn't we cast the demon out?" They were confused because they'd been successfully casting out devils and this had been the first time they'd come across a demon that they could not cast out. Howbeit, Jesus cast it out with ease. He said to them, "This kind only comes out by fasting and prayer." What did He mean by "this kind?" Jesus wasn't necessarily dealing with the rank of the spirit, He was dealing with the legality, even though the spirit may have possibly been a high-ranking spirit. He was dealing with the legal grounds that the demon had been standing on. How so? Think of the gulf that divided the street in my dream. Now, think of a family of witches who have been consulting with demonic spirits for generations on end. Every time a witch consults with a demon, that witch enters into an agreement with that spirit. This is why witches and warlocks are referred to as mediums. The word "medium" simply means "something in a middle position" (Source: Merriam Webster). She essentially stands between both roads; she stands in the gulf, acting as a bridge or a halfway point between both dimensions. But in doing so, she causes herself to be bound because she's crossed a boundary. But again, think of a family of witches that enter into an agreement with a network of demonic forces. This agreement is pretty much a contract. If you've ever gotten a loan before, you should know that the lender will hand you a very lengthy contract, printed out on several pages. In that moment, you were likely so desperate to get the money being offered that you completely ignored the small print or you didn't necessarily understand the legal jargon. Honestly, you didn't care to understand it. You just wanted to circumvent the process. As the agent took you through each page, he or she tried to explain and summarize the text in a matter of seconds. After that, the agent said, "Sign here. Initial here. Date here." You didn't think too much of it because you wanted that process to be over with. You wanted to get that check or that direct deposit as quickly as you could. After you were done, the agent handed you a check or deposited the money into your account. You shook hands with the agent and walked out of the company excited, relieved and energized. The money solved a very-present problem that you had, but later on, it created other problems. Please note that taking a loan is simply means that you are borrowing or taking from your future. This is why God tells us to be anxious for nothing. Impatience is the breeding grounds for witchcraft. There's small print or things you don't necessarily understand anytime you consult with a witch or you read your horoscope. Please understand that it is an exchange, and most of the people who involve themselves in these practices are confused as to why they keep dealing with the issues that seem to plague them. Most people bound by the enemy have absolutely NO CLUE as to why they keep falling into the same traps that their parents and grandparents fell into. They don't know why they can't keep a job, why they keep dating the same devil in a different person or why they have so many health issues. It may be a legality! This is why I often tell people to fast and pray whenever they see cycles in their lives! Cycles represent bottomless pits; they are never-ending loops, rotations or events that have to be addressed. Again, think of a family of witches who've been consulting with demonic forces for several generations. What they've done is not only given themselves to the enemy, but they've committed their children to the enemy as well, either knowingly or unknowingly. In that family, you will see a lot of premature death, mental illnesses, physical illnesses, promiscuity, divorce, familial division, barrenness and a host of other curses. Let's say that four generations later, a young man is born, but he is given up for adoption. His new family raises him in the fear and admonition of the Lord. However, there's still a price tag over his head; he's still spiraling down the same pit that his parents, grandparents and great-grandparents were in.

One day, he goes to the altar for deliverance after dealing with a host of problems from sexual perversion to rage. While at the altar, he begins to laugh hysterically and a strange voice comes out of his mouth. "I'm not coming out," the demon whispers seductively before laughing again. "I have a legal right to him!" What does this mean? Of course, in most instances, the unclean spirit may be lying, but in other cases, the spirit may be using legal gibberish. In other words, the young man is a part of an agreement made between his ancestors and a host of familiar spirits. To end this agreement, he may have to fast and pray. He has to repent; this means to turn or renounce his ancestors' witchcraft and call on the name of Jesus. So, the young man who the disciples had trouble casting the devil out of was more than likely a part of a legal agreement. Someone in his family line may have been practicing idolatry or playing with witchcraft. All the same, the demonic entity could outrank the person who's trying to cast it out. When this happens, the minister should step aside and allow someone else to conduct the deliverance. If there is no one else present, the minister may have to fast and pray. Again, this is why Jesus told the disciples, "This kind comes out only through fasting and prayer."

Sexual Boundaries

One of the most interesting dreams I can remember having took place in 2009. I was living in Germany at that time. Anyhow, I dreamed that I was standing on the side of a lone road talking to around three or four women. We were obviously in Europe somewhere because we were surrounded by rolling hills. I couldn't see any buildings or structures for miles on end.

While we were talking, I saw the women look past me, and without warning, they started lowering their heads. I wondered why they were looking fearful as if they were trying to avoid eye contact with someone, but before I could turn fully around, I saw this guy approaching us. I remember him having a dark complexion and wearing sunglasses. He was maybe around 5'7 and he had a somewhat small to medium build. He walked up to every woman and took away her cellphone. Each woman lowered her head all the more whenever he approached her. Additionally, none of the women had resisted him. He'd stolen something from all of them, but to stay safe, they didn't open their mouths or lift their heads. I remember looking at each woman in awe, surprised that none of them had put up a fight. Finally, it was my turn. I was holding my cell phone in my hand, and the guy walked up and took my phone out of my hand. I yelled at him and told him I was going to call the cops, and then, I took my phone back. He was unusually calm. "So, you're going to call the cops on me?" he countered. I emphatically said "yes," before dialing 911. Not long after that, the cops arrived and the scene switched. I found myself standing a distance away from my attacker who, at that time, was being questioned by a couple of cops. We were still standing next to a road, surrounded by hills, but I was now further down. I saw them hand him a few papers, and I understood it to mean that he would eventually go to court for his crimes, but he wasn't being arrested at that moment. I was livid, but more than that, I was terrified. The women I'd been speaking with were afraid of him, so I knew I was about to be in that fight … alone! As the cops pulled off, I began to run. I could see him pursuing me in the distance. I ran from one house to another, trying to hide from the guy, and the owners would let me in; they were in full support of my views, but whenever he'd find his way to their homes, they'd tell on me or ask me to leave. I'd end up on the run again, and this went on until I woke up.

After waking up from that dream, I wrote an article, created a website and published the article on the website. I think the website was www.spiritofwhoredom.info. Of course, I've since taken that website down because I eventually moved on to something else, but I used the website to share my article and what I believed the dream meant. I also wrote a book immediately after having this dream, but I don't think I detailed the dream in the book. That book is entitled, "The Spirit of Heaviness and All its Cousins."

But what did that dream mean? It was a two-dimensional dream, detailing both my past and my future. Before I'd gotten saved, I'd once been a man trap or better yet, a seductress. After I wholeheartedly surrendered my heart to God, I renounced premarital sex, and not long after that, I denounced it, meaning, I made my declaration not only a public declaration, but I took a brazen stance against sexual immorality. This is because, in order for me to get free, I had to study, study and study some more. I had to learn what sex was outside of the context in which I knew it, and what God's original purpose for it was. I had to learn what premarital sex was, what it did and look at the toll it had taken on my life (I'd had two failed marriages and a whole lot of soulish wounds because of those poor choices). It dealt with my future because in the dream, I wasn't just talking with the women, I was ministering to them. How do I know this? Because they were standing around listening to me and seemingly asking questions. They were all facing me and they were very attentive. Nevertheless, when that dark spirit walked up disguised as a man, it began to rob each and everyone of them, stealing from them what it had once stole from me—my voice. In the dream, the thief had taken my phone from me just as he'd taken their phones away from them. Keep in mind, we were in the middle of nowhere. We were surrounded by rolling hills, so our phones were our only source of communication with the world at large. The women had all been engaging before he'd walked up, but when he'd come, they'd all closed their mouths, dropped their heads and loosened their grips on their phones. And just like he'd done with them, the devil took something from me, but unlike the women in the dream, I'd taken it back. This was a prophetic picture of my future. At the time when I had the dream, I hadn't fully taken my voice back. All the same, I found myself on the run, hiding from that spirit with no help because it was hellbent on retaliation. It had its sights on me, and no woman in that desolate place was willing to put herself at risk trying to help me.

But what was I fighting? First and foremost, I neglected to mention that the man looked familiar. I don't remember who he looked like to me, but I do remember that he looked extremely familiar. This normally indicates that the spirit in question is a familiar spirit. Next, why was I only dreaming about women? Why was the guy attacking women? Because women are the largest part of my assignment. This reminds me of another dream I'd had a few years later, where I was in a small room surrounded by women. I was ministering to them, but more in a casual way (it wasn't a formal setup; it was more like a gathering of friends or acquaintances). All of a sudden, a woman came into the room and told me that I was about to go on the air. I looked at her and then, told her that I wasn't ready yet. My hair was a mess. I wanted someone to add some extensions to my hair, but the woman replied, "No time!" She told me that I was about to go on the air in a few minutes and they had someone who would style my natural hair and do my makeup. I remember feeling insecure in the dream as she rushed me into another room, where she sat me in a chair. Immediately, another woman walked up and started styling my hair. In that dream, I was surrounded by women. Why? Because the same devil that had attacked me had attacked many of them. Let me explain.

I'd dealt with a lot of "sexual attacks" as a child and as a young woman. Consequently, when I stepped out into the world as a young woman, I didn't know who I was or how to behave like a respectable woman. It is for this reason that I became promiscuous. I went from one relationship to the other, giving myself away and thinking that what I was doing was normal. *Note: it was normal in the world.* All the same, it was normal for me. I had been surrounded by promiscuous people my entire life! I didn't know what a whole and healthy relationship looked like outside of The Cosby Show (which I RARELY watched) or one of those shows on Nickelodeon that I loved to watch. When I got saved (at the age of 20), I was still partying and fornicating. Honestly, even after getting saved, it took me nearly a decade to fully surrender my life to Christ. People are often shocked when I tell them that I got delivered from fornication while married. Yes, married! If this shocks you, chances are, you have an erroneous idea of what fornication is, and that's okay. Most Christians don't truly, wholeheartedly understand fornication. It just sounds like a religious word that simply means no sex! But years after having that dream, God was using me to write a book entitled *Wise Her Still* (I'm not sure if it was the first edition or *Wise Her Still Too,* the second edition). What I do remember is that I was living in Florida, married to my second husband

and I'd finally surrendered my life to God. I don't know what I was writing in the book, but I do remember that there was some revelation that God shared with me that made me stand to my feet and begin to weep. I suddenly had a God's-eye-view of fornication, and when I saw it the way He saw it, my heart broke. I stood to my feet and began to repent loudly. "Lord, I'm sorry!" I said. "I didn't know, Lord! I didn't know!" What did God share with me?

1. **Fornication isn't an act; it's a heart condition.** The heart condition is the result of each person's personal beliefs, and our personal beliefs are made up of what we know, our experiences and what we took from those experiences. All the same, a wrongful mindset is the result of a lack of knowledge. So, even as a married woman, I still had a heart of fornication (before that event), meaning, had my ex and I divorced at that time, chances are, I would have fornicated with the next potential husband. God wasn't interested in me being abstinent, He wanted me to agree with Him about love, marriage and sex. Abstinence would then be a by-product or a fruit of that agreement, meaning, I wouldn't just be refraining from premarital sex because it's the right thing to do, I'd be refraining from premarital sex because I no longer agreed with it. James 2:18 reads, 'But someone will say, 'You have faith, and I have works.' Show me your faith without your works, and I will show you my faith by my works.'" We all know that faith without works is dead; it has no life, movement

or power. Faith is demonstrated in our works, but when we do the works without having faith, our works become mere performances. They are religious demonstrations, and this is okay—for a short period of time, after all, perfect love or, better yet, mature love casts out fear. Religiousness is oftentimes the product of fear, but as we mature in Christ, our works or demonstrations are no longer the products of fear and religiousness, but we'll make the right choices simply because we love the Lord. This is why God said in John 14:15, "If ye love me, keep my commandments." He's not referencing the Old Testament when He says "commandments," but instead, the Lord is referencing Matthew 22:37-40, which reads, "Jesus said unto him, Thou shalt love the Lord thy God with all thy heart, and with all thy soul, and with all thy mind. This is the first and great commandment. And the second is like unto it, Thou shalt love thy neighbor as thyself. On these two commandments hang all the law and the prophets." So, in short, I learned that the fruit of fornication had everything to do with the state or condition of my heart. If I wanted to change my fruit, I had to uproot the lies and all of the seeds that the enemy had planted in my heart when I had been broken, perverted and ignorant. I then had to replace those seeds with the Word of God, and be patient with God as He sent people to water those seeds.

2. **Sex induces intimacy, but it is not intimacy.** Sex is God's way of explaining intimacy. Whenever a man

and a woman come together to have a sexual encounter, they will remove some, if not all of their clothes. This means they reveal their nakedness to one another. This is vulnerability. Once they lie down together, this is another stage or level of vulnerability because it typically involves a level of trust. When lying down, a woman (the weaker vessel) is almost defenseless. Additionally, when she's naked, she's vulnerable and exposed. True intimacy is the revealing of the heart; nothing hidden, nothing withheld. It is getting naked before God, showing Him every detail of who you are, and submitting all of your brokenness, fears, secrets, insecurities and flaws to Him. This requires full-blown trust in the Lord. When a woman engages in sex outside of the marital covenant, she's opening her legs because she neglected to guard her heart. The Bible tells us to guard our hearts, for out of them pour the issues of life. She didn't cast down evil imaginations and every high thing that exalts itself against the knowledge of God, nor did she bring every thought into captivity and make it obey Christ. Instead, she allowed those imaginations of intimacy or a greater connection with the man she believes she loves to intensify or she allowed her fear of losing him to get the best of her. Either way, she's trying to create a deeper connection with the man by submitting her body to him, but here's the problem. If she's willing to have sex outside of marriage, chances are, her heart is not ready to be revealed. She doesn't fully know who she is at that moment, so she's revealing something that should have been concealed and developed more. The same is true for the man, of course. The Bible tells husbands to love their wives as they love themselves. A man who truly knows himself can love himself, and a man who truly loves himself wouldn't give his body away so freely. Just like a child is too immature and underdeveloped to engage in sexual activity, the same is true for a babe in Christ. Children don't know their bodies; immature believers don't know their identities. And it is for this reason that most relationships that start wrong don't survive the fire-test or the tests of time. What is the fire-test? 1 Corinthians 3:13-15 answers this question. "Every man's work shall be made manifest: for the day shall declare it, because it shall be revealed by fire; and the fire shall try every man's work of what sort it is. If any man's work abide which he hath built thereupon, he shall receive a reward. If any man's work shall be burned, he shall suffer loss: but he himself shall be saved; yet so as by fire." The Lord tests every structure we build with fire. Satan also tests those structures. If those structures are not sound—if they are not secured by the Word of God and faith, the day of adversity will likely prove to be too much for the relationship to stand.

3. **Sex does not equate to love.** Sex was never designed to be a tool to get a man or a woman to love

you all the more or to reward that person for loving you; sex was designed to represent intimacy. Through our marriages and through sex within the context of a Godly marriage, we would come to understand and respect intimacy with God all the more. God gets pleasure when we worship Him. He loves when we open our hearts to Him and tell Him everything—even the stuff we're ashamed to talk about. He loves when we spend intimate time with Him, just loving on Him and releasing beautiful sounds of worship. Just like we get pleasure when we're intimate with one another, God gets pleasure from our intimacy, but it's a different type of pleasure obviously. This is why He said that those who worship Him must worship Him in Spirit and in Truth. Howbeit, when sex is used inappropriately (outside the context of marriage to induce or seduce a person into loving us, marrying us or doing whatsoever it is that we want that person to do), it becomes a tool of manipulation, a wile or an extension of witchcraft. Anytime you try to bend the will of another human being, you are operating in witchcraft. Witchcraft brings a person under the influence of another person, but they eventually sober up.

4. **Mature love requires mature people.** The Bible says, "Don't awaken love before its time." The Berean Study Bible says it this way, "O daughters of Jerusalem, I adjure you: Do not arouse or awaken love until the time is right" (Song of Solomon 8:4). The

Bible references what God calls "perfect love." The word "perfect" in this context doesn't mean without flaw. It simply means "mature love." To have mature love, you have to have mature lovers. Galatians 4:1-2 reads, "Now I say, That the heir, as long as he is a child, differeth nothing from a servant, though he be lord of all; but is under tutors and governors until the time appointed of the father. Even so we, when we were children, were in bondage under the elements of the world." In this scripture, the word "child" isn't necessarily dealing with age, it's dealing with maturity. It pretty much says that the heir (which all believers are), as long as he or she is immature is no different than a slave, meaning, that person thinks, reasons and behaves like a slave. A slave of what, you ask? The elements of this world, meaning, the individual is subject to and enslaved by his or her own carnality. What happens when you awaken love before its time? Two immature people prematurely reveal their underdeveloped hearts to one another, but all too often not before revealing themselves physically to one another. Over time, they find themselves growing more and more displeased with one another since immature people are naturally selfish and somewhat narcissistic. Because they are in bondage to the elements of this world, they continue to use carnal things in their attempts to control, seduce, please or hurt one another. They do this until the relationship finally gives up its ghost or it becomes more and more perverted. Whatever you feed will grow; whatever you starve will die. The same is true for sexual perversion. Slowly, but surely, the couple becomes less and less intimate (in communication because they don't like one another's hearts), but they try to overcompensate for this lack of love for one another using sex. The problem is, the human being is wired to like sex, but sex without true intimacy of the heart then becomes nothing but performance. It becomes more and more about self-gratification or manipulating the other person until one or both parties in the relationship is no longer interested in it. This is oftentimes because that person is caught up in the throngs of a new relationship and they haven't closed off their hearts to one another yet. They are still getting to know one another, which means that the sexual encounter between both parties will likely be more heightened and have more significance or, at least, it'll feel that way.

5. **No sex before marriage!** Sex outside of the confines of marriage, in 99.9% of the cases, will likely involve two people who are not yet mature enough to be married; this is especially true if it is a repeated event between the couple. In other words, after "messing up," they continued to have sex with one another, chances are, they are trying to strengthen their relationship and appease one another's sexual lusts. This is a deviation from what God designed us to do and how He designed us to think. In this case, neither

of the parties involved truly know what love is; they are oxytocin addicts. They still think that love has everything to do with sharing moonlit walks on the beach, holding hands, staring one another in the eyes and passionately kissing each other, all the while, indulging in the endorphins released every time they illegally cross a boundary with one another. In other words, they are deceived and not operating out of a sober mind. At some point in their relationship, their brains won't release the endorphins that they once released when they kissed one another, held hands or shared a bed. At some point, responsibility enters the picture, and it is then that the couple has to start investing what is most important to them into maintaining the relationship. For example, the man may not be able to hang out with his friends like he used to or the woman probably won't be able to spend money the way she used to spend it. This is the lust-love test. It is during this time that 99 percent of relationships built on erroneous beliefs give up their ghosts. The relationships don't necessarily fail; they simply bow down and acknowledge that the Word of God is true.

Let's look at the history of sex and God's original design for it.

Genesis 1:26-28: And God said, Let us make man in our image, after our likeness: and let them have dominion over the fish of the sea, and over the fowl of the air, and over the cattle, and over all the earth, and over every creeping thing that creepeth upon the earth. So God created man in his own image, in the image of God created he him; male and female created he them. And God blessed them, and God said unto them, Be fruitful, and multiply, and replenish the earth, and subdue it: and have dominion over the fish of the sea, and over the fowl of the air, and over every living thing that moveth upon the earth.

Genesis 2:4-7: These are the generations of the heavens and of the earth when they were created, in the day that the LORD God made the earth and the heavens, and every plant of the field before it was in the earth, and every herb of the field before it grew: for the LORD God had not caused it to rain upon the earth, and there was not a man to till the ground. But there went up a mist from the earth, and watered the whole face of the ground. And the LORD God formed man of the dust of the ground, and breathed into his nostrils the breath of life; and man became a living soul.

Genesis 2:15: And the LORD God took the man, and put him into the garden of Eden to dress it and to keep it.

Genesis 2:21-25: And the LORD God caused a deep sleep to fall upon Adam, and he slept: and he took one of his ribs, and closed up the flesh instead thereof; and the rib, which the LORD God had taken from man, made he a woman, and brought her unto the man. And Adam said, This is now bone

Sexual Boundaries

of my bones, and flesh of my flesh: she shall be called Woman, because she was taken out of Man. Therefore shall a man leave his father and his mother, and shall cleave unto his wife: and they shall be one flesh. And they were both naked, the man and his wife, and were not ashamed.

Genesis 4:1: And Adam knew Eve his wife; and she conceived, and bare Cain, and said, I have gotten a man from the LORD.

Let's fast forward a little to the Mosaic Law. Marriage in the Old Testament involved:
1. Contract (Ketubbah)
2. Consummation (Chuppah)
3. Ceremony (The Wedding Feast)

Most marriages in the biblical era had been arranged. In other words, the bride had little to no say regarding who she would marry. In many instances, she would be given the opportunity to express her interest, approval or disdain for a man. But for the most part, because of their honor for their father, many (if not most) women married the men their fathers either picked for them or approved for them. If the daughter wasn't interested, of course, the father would reject the man's proposal. Marriage, in that time, was seen as more of an agreement between families, rather than an agreement between the husband and the wife. Once a man expressed interest in a woman, the father of the bride-to-be would have to accept the man's proposal to marry his daughter or reject it. If the father accepted the proposal, the father and the potential groom would enter into a marital contract called a ketubbah. But before they signed this contract, the father would discuss the dowry with the man, and if the man agreed, the contract was then presented to him. The minute both parties signed that contract (the father and the groom), the woman was (culturally and legally) considered to be the property of the groom. Today, we would say that the couple was engaged, but back then, they didn't practice the traditions that we practice today. In other words, the minute a man signed the ketubbah, the couple was seen as married, even though they hadn't officially married or consummated their marriage. This is because our modern-day understanding of marriage is completely disconnected from what the Jews considered marriage to be in the biblical days. Marriage was and is an agreement between two sound authorities. The father of the bride, being of a sound mind, would agree to allow the groom-to-be, who was also (supposed to be) of a sound mind to not just marry his daughter, but to marry into his family. You see, a man's name in that day and era was directly connected to his wealth and his reputation, so if a man allowed his daughter to marry into a broken, perverted and rebellious family, he could ruin his reputation for generations to come. This would directly impact and affect his wealth and how society treated his family.

The groom-to-be would then have the responsibility of providing his new father-in-law with the dowry, which was

oftentimes pretty steep. The purpose of the dowry was:
1. To provide the father with the wages or earnings that he would lose once his daughter left his home. Most men at that time were farmers. Their sons and daughters worked for them everyday (except on the Sabbath day). They weren't just working for their father, they were generating wealth or, better yet, a legacy for the sons. When a daughter left home, the father would be losing that extra hand, which meant that he'd be also losing money. The dowry compensated him for those lost wages.
2. It was also seen as a gift from the groom or the groom's family to the bride's family.
3. It established trust between both families.
4. It chased away the men of questionable and immoral character.
5. If a woman was later widowed, the money would go to her to care for her and her children; this ensured that she would not end up destitute.

After the dowry (also called a mohar) was paid, the bride-to-be would remain at home with her father for up to a year while her groom went to prepare a place for her; this place was called the wedding chamber. She didn't know when her "fiance'" would come to get her and consummate their marriage. Instead, she had to make sure that she was ready at all times. This meant she had to keep oil in her lamps at all times and her maidens had to also keep oil in their lamps. The groom would often come like a thief in the night.

One night, the groom-to-be would gather up his "best men" and they would make their way towards the bride's house. As they neared the bride's home, the men would shout and blow a shofar to let her know that they were near. The people in her community would often rise from their beds and come outside because of all of the ruckus. They would then shout, "The bridegroom is coming!" When the bride heard this, she would rise out of her bed and start getting ready with the help of her maidens. Once the groom arrived, he would gather up his bride and take her to the place he'd prepared for her, but before he did, her father would hand her or one of the witnesses a white sheet. This sheet is what we refer to as a "purity cloth." The purpose of the purity cloth was to prove or disprove that the bride was a virgin. In Jewish tradition, they understood the complexity of sex; it wasn't just two people having harmless fun. They took the biblical definition of sex to heart (and rightfully so); they understood that when a man lied down with a woman, the two people were now one person. This doesn't mean that they ceased to exist individually. It meant that in God's eyes, the two souls had merged, and no man could break this connection apart. The couple would then go into the wedding chamber while their witnesses stood outside, waiting for the groom to reappear. He would leave the chamber briefly to assure everyone that the consummation had taken place and his bride was indeed a virgin. The bloodstained sheet would be the evidence, and it was put away to protect the bride and her father against any false accusations from the groom. For seven days, the couple would remain in the wedding chamber, and when they emerged, the wedding party would celebrate. This is when they would begin the ceremony or the wedding celebration.

What can we take from this? First off, marriage has never been two people standing at an altar, exchanging vows. This is our traditional, westernized modern-day version of marriage. Marriage in the biblical era was all about agreement, just as it is today, even though most people don't understand this. This is why most divorces are filed on the grounds of "irreconcilable differences" meaning the couple cannot seem to agree, especially on the issues that are most important. Howbeit, it was never supposed to be this way. The father protected his daughter by examining and testing the groom-to-be. And if a groom suddenly rose up and asked for a divorce, it wasn't easy for him to get it back in those days because he had to prove that his wife had been "unclean" before he'd married her. This is a breach in the contract between him and her father. This also meant that by accusing the wife of "playing the whore," the man was also accusing the father of the bride; he was essentially saying that the father was immoral, dishonest and untrustworthy. This could affect the father in so many ways, and it is for this reason that the father would then present the bloodstained cloth at the divorce proceedings, proving that his daughter had been a virgin and that his son-in-law had simply had a change of heart towards her. This would prove the son-in-law to be immoral, dishonest and rebellious, and consequently, he would have to pay a bride-price.

Sexual Boundaries

Deuteronomy 22:13-19 details this event. "If any man take a wife, and go in unto her, and hate her, and give occasions of speech against her, and bring up an evil name upon her, and say, I took this woman, and when I came to her, I found her not a maid: Then shall the father of the damsel, and her mother, take and bring forth the tokens of the damsel's virginity unto the elders of the city in the gate: And the damsel's father shall say unto the elders, I gave my daughter unto this man to wife, and he hateth her; and, lo, he hath given occasions of speech against her, saying, I found not thy daughter a maid; and yet these are the tokens of my daughter's virginity. And they shall spread the cloth before the elders of the city. And the elders of that city shall take that man and chastise him; and they shall amerce him in an hundred shekels of silver, and give them unto the father of the damsel, because he hath brought up an evil name upon a virgin of Israel: and she shall be his wife; he may not put her away all his days."

It happened then just as it happens now. A man could have sex with a woman and suddenly begin to despise her. Think about a steak dinner at an expensive restaurant. Some immoral, money-loving guy could walk into a restaurant and eat a five-hundred dollar steak dinner. After he's eaten eighty-percent of the steak, he could call the waitress or waiter over and begin to complain. "This steak tasted awful! Plus, the salad was old! I'm not paying for this!" Now, in some cheap restaurants, he may be able to get out of paying his bill, but most restaurants would look at the amount of food he consumed and then, they would likely decide that he has to pay full price for the food he's eaten. This is because they know that he's simply trying to get out of his responsibility to them. And while women are far greater and far more important than a steak dinner, the concept is similar. Again, a man could have sex with his bride and suddenly change his mind about her. The problem with this is, the minute he sleeps with her, she's no longer considered a single woman. In the biblical era, she was seen as married or defiled. Again, the goal is to understand God's original design and purpose for sex. Let's look further into the scriptures about Old Testament marriages since history helps us to understand the present and it gives us a snapshot of the future.

Verse	Scripture
Deuteronomy 22:13-19	If any man takes a wife and goes in to her and then hates her and accuses her of misconduct and brings a bad name upon her, saying, 'I took this woman, and when I came near her, I did not find in her evidence of virginity,' then the father of the young woman and her mother shall take and bring out the evidence of her virginity to the elders of the city in the gate. And the father of the young woman shall say to the elders, 'I gave my daughter to this man to marry, and he

	hates her; and behold, he has accused her of misconduct, saying, "I did not find in your daughter evidence of virginity." And yet this is the evidence of my daughter's virginity.' And they shall spread the cloak before the elders of the city. Then the elders of that city shall take the man and whip him, and they shall fine him a hundred shekels of silver and give them to the father of the young woman, because he has brought a bad name upon a virgin of Israel. And she shall be his wife. He may not divorce her all his days.
Deuteronomy 22:20-21	But if the thing is true, that evidence of virginity was not found in the young woman, then they shall bring out the young woman to the door of her father's house, and the men of her city shall stone her to death with stones, because she has done an outrageous thing in Israel by whoring in her father's house. So you shall purge the evil from your midst.

As we look at history, it would appear that women have been sold as property, mishandled and mistreated since the beginning of time, and while this may be true in some instances, for the most part, Jewish tradition was centered around protecting the woman (the weaker vessel). God knows something that we don't know, and that is—marriage is more than just two people who love each other and decide that they want to spend their lives together. Marriage is an agreement between two authorities; it is an agreement that is sealed with blood. This means it's a covenant, and the difference between a standard contract and a covenant is this—anything established with blood can only be dissolved with blood. This is why we needed (and still need) the blood of Jesus. You see, when Adam consummated his marriage with Eve, they were both "fallen." This meant that every child born to them would be born in this pit or ditch; they would be born in a fallen state. To redeem mankind, blood needed to be shed, so before Christ came into the Earth, the Jewish priests had to sacrifice bulls, rams, goats, turtledoves and other animals as a means for purification. Eventually, Jesus came into the Earth to settle the debt owed; He paid the price for our sins. In other words, He established a new covenant, and because of His blood, we are no longer under the Mosaic Law.

Before we go any further, let's publish a few facts:
1. Traditional weddings as we know them didn't start until the 19th century. Before then, couples rarely married for love. Western marriages were more about power and privilege than they were about love.
2. The word "maiden" means virgin. This means that the phrase "maiden name" means your virgin name; it is

the name given to a woman by her father. When a man agrees with the father to marry a woman, he pretty much gives her his name; this is the "canopy" that legalizes his right to lie with her. When a woman has sex while wearing her father's name, she essentially dishonors her father.
3. Dating is a worldly concept. It allows men to "experience" several women before settling down with one woman. It promotes promiscuity and instability. Courting, on the other hand, is about marriage. It simply means that, because of his honor, love and the fear of God, a man agrees with the Father in Heaven to pursue marriage. It means that he'll take the necessary steps and precautions to ensure that he not only refrains from dishonoring God by having sex with a woman, it also means that he refrains from dishonoring her father. Any man who is willing to dishonor God is not ready for marriage or, at least, he's not ready for marriage the way God designed it to operate. He may be ready for his idea of marriage, but ideas change over time.

So, what then is sex? Sex is the joining together of two people in body; this represents the uniting of their minds in agreement. Eve wasn't created until:
1. Adam had a job. His assignment was to till the ground.
2. Adam had a home. God placed him in the Garden of Eden.

3. Adam could hear from God. God tested him by bringing all the animals of the Earth to him to see what he would call them. When he passed this test, God put him to sleep and brought Eve out of him.

Eve's assignment was to be a help-meet; the same is true for women. God designed us to be help-meets. Now, this may sound offensive to someone who's been hurt by men, abandoned by men and taken advantage of by men—or raised by women who've been hurt and rejected by men. But you would have to know and see God's heart to understand how and why He designed us (women) the way He did. He didn't have anything malicious in mind. As a matter of fact, He established those laws to protect women! Being a help-meet is a blessing, but only if a woman is paired up with a man who knows what he needs help with. In other words, he needs to know who he is in Christ and what his purpose is. Not only should he know this, but he should be in full agreement with the Father, just as the bride-to-be should be in agreement with the Father. This is what allows for a Godly, healthy and impenetrable union. Of course, if you're like me, you may then say, "I'm not a virgin! Does this disqualify me for marriage?!" It depends on who you ask! By religious people, you'd be disqualified if you were molested, raped or had sex before you were saved. This would make more than fifty percent of women ineligible for marriage. Religion doesn't teach the context or concept of marriage in God's eyes, and anytime I come across someone who comes from a strict religious background, I oftentimes ask them a single question. I ask, "Before you married your spouse, were you a virgin?" Most of them won't answer this question; instead, they'll ask me, "What does that have to do with anything?" And for the single ones, I ask, "Are you a virgin? Cause, if not, you have been married, so by your legalistic understanding of the scriptures, you too are disqualified from marriage." Legalism causes people to filter scriptures through their modern-day understanding of the Bible without knowing or understanding history or what it means "to die" in God's eyes. If I went by their understanding, I would have been disqualified long ago because I was molested as a child and raped when I was ten-years old. I would be the "property" of my rapist, or I would have to be dragged to my father's house and stoned on the front steps.

There was one significant difference between a standard agreement and a covenant. A covenant was an agreement that could only be established and broken by the shedding of blood. A daughter carried her father's blood, so in order for a man to marry her, he had to honor the father enough to enter into an agreement with the father, and when the time came, he would shed her blood on the purity cloth. This established a covenant between the two that could only be nullified by the shedding of more blood (fornication, death). A covenant, in layman's terms, is an agreement between two or more people that has been established by the shedding of blood or the word of a father; this was the equivalent of a signed and dated contract. This agreement could only be broken through the shedding of blood or if one of the parties was already a part of another agreement. If the woman was not a virgin when the man consummated his marriage with her, his contract with her father would be nullified because she had already been joined to another man, even if the father had been unaware of her indiscretions. While no agreement between her lover and her father had been established, her blood had been shed. This is like Target selling you an open bag of potato chips; it sounds harsh, but this was the way it was looked upon. This would make it illegal for another guy to touch her unless the man she'd slept with had passed away. In death, his blood is shed. What is more powerful than sex is the power of agreement. This is why so many people today are bound. Agreements aren't voided just because we fall out of love with someone or just because two people no longer agree. Marriages are legally broken when the husband is no longer in agreement with God. His disagreement with God will oftentimes manifest in his inability to agree with his wife. For example, if a man decides that he wants to have an extramarital affair, he is not only contending with his wife, but his real fight is with God. This means that he is in breach of his contract with God, after all, God told husbands to love their wives as they love themselves. Additionally, in Luke 10:27 says, "And he answering said, Thou shalt love the Lord thy God with all thy heart, and with all thy soul, and with all thy strength, and with all thy mind; and thy neighbor as thyself." In John 14:15, the Lord said, "If ye love me, keep my commandments." So, the binding agent in every marital union has to be God, for God is love! Let me explain it this way. When a man loves God

Sexual Boundaries

with all of his heart, soul and strength, he will automatically honor God since honor is an extension of worship. Because of his love and honor for God, he will forsake the lustful desires of his flesh and seek to please the Lord in all that he does. Will temptation come his way? Yes, of course! Howbeit, just like Joseph rejected Potiphar's wife because of his love and fear of God, so will a man who has chosen to honor God with everything he has (his mind, body, treasures, etc.). Nevertheless, if he ceases to trust and believe God, but his wife is a believer (or vice versa), according to 1 Corinthians 7:12, she shouldn't leave him. However, if the unbeliever wants to depart, the Bible says to let that person depart. But if he sheds the blood of another woman in adultery, he has not only violated his agreement with God, but he has also violated his agreement with his wife. This is why she has the legal right to walk away—should she choose to do so.

Understand this—where there is no legal covenant, you will always find a coven or the grouping/clotting together of broken like-minded individuals! Let me explain it this way. Back in the biblical days, it was commonplace for a king to have several wives and several concubines, but one queen. A concubine was a little higher than a slave, but lower than a wife. She received the responsibilities of a wife, but not the benefits. A concubine had no voice; she could not make any decisions regarding her children, the running of the castle, etc. Concubines were often grouped together in what is traditionally called a harem. Merriam Webster defines a

harem as:
- the wives, concubines, female relatives, and servants occupying a harem
- informal: a group of women associated with one man

This is similar to a coven. A coven, according to Merriam Webster, is:
- a collection of individuals with similar interests or activities
- an assembly or band of usually 13 witches

Another way of describing a coven is a group of women without a proper covering! And notice that I used the term "clotting together." Think about blood. When blood is healthy, it freely flows to the area that it's supposed to flow to, and it also extracts and transfers the nutrients and blood cells needed to that area. But when an injury takes place or when a person is wounded, blood often clots together to stop the person from bleeding to death! This is why you should never be in a rush to fit in! Sometimes, a group of men or women who are pooling together are not hanging out because they are great friends, they are clotting together because they are wounded! Notice that anytime you've gotten your heart broken, there was an insatiable and almost unquenchable desire and need for you to call a group of your friends, especially if you are a woman. But you weren't going to call the healed, happy and functional friends. No, you called the dysfunctional, broken friends who were still swinging at the air because some man or woman hurt them a long time ago! You just gave them the opportunity to finally land a few licks before they retreated back to swinging at the air. This is called clotting!

So, what then is sex? It's an agreement, but just like you wouldn't enter into a contractual agreement without first understanding the terms of that agreement, you shouldn't enter into anyone's bedroom outside of a legal, God-established marital covenant because you don't know the fine print behind the individual. This is why there are so many one-parent homes, divorces and broken people on the market today. Most people see sex as a casual fling with no repercussions, but this isn't true. When two people lie down together, they become one in God's eyes. Blood is shed and a covenant is established. They can go their separate ways, but they are still essentially connected; this is why you'll notice that many women, for example, tend to be attracted to men who remind them of one of their exes.

Today, many men and women are soul tied to a bunch of folks, and honestly, they cannot and have not figured out why they can't seem to progress forward. But this has everything to do with the agreements that they are a part of. This is why God established boundaries around our sexuality. Sexual purity isn't just for women, it's also for men. But when we dishonor God by not loving Him with all of our hearts, strength and minds, we'll go out there and sleep with people in our attempts to fill a God-sized void in our hearts. Let's revisit the dream I spoke of. Again, I was standing on a hill, surrounded by a few women. They were all facing me. It was a beautiful sunny day, and we were surrounded by rolling hills and landscape. All of the women were smiling. The joy radiating from their faces was as bright as the sun; that is, until they saw a dark figure in the distance. In that moment, they dropped their heads. The head represents authority. They also closed their mouths. The voice represents identity. The thief walked up and stole something right out of their hands. The hand represents agreement. He didn't do this behind their backs when they were looking away. He was facing them, and they were facing him. Again, this represents a form of agreement called compliance. Because of fear, they kept their heads low while he robbed them of their identities, their futures and their happiness. And when I stood up on, not just my own behalf, but their behalves, they all betrayed me because they were more concerned with living a "normal life" than they were with recovering their voices and their identities. The dark figure never caught me. And years later, I would find myself having a series of dreams about me being rescued and delivered. I soon discovered that deliverance is for the hungry; it's for the desperate, and the reason so many people don't get it is because they aren't hungry enough.

God placed boundaries around us for a reason. Understand that sexual boundaries are designed to protect, not just your body, but your voice. Tamar had been raped by her brother Amnon. The Bible tells us that he was so stricken with her that he fell ill. Let's briefly look at that story.

Sexual Boundaries

2 Samuel 13:1-19

And it came to pass after this, that Absalom the son of David had a fair sister, whose name was Tamar; and Amnon the son of David loved her. And Amnon was so vexed, that he fell sick for his sister Tamar; for she was a virgin; and Amnon thought it hard for him to do any thing to her. But Amnon had a friend, whose name was Jonadab, the son of Shimeah David's brother: and Jonadab was a very subtil man. And he said unto him, Why art thou, being the king's son, lean from day to day? wilt thou not tell me? And Amnon said unto him, I love Tamar, my brother Absalom's sister. And Jonadab said unto him, Lay thee down on thy bed, and make thyself sick: and when thy father cometh to see thee, say unto him, I pray thee, let my sister Tamar come, and give me meat, and dress the meat in my sight, that I may see it, and eat it at her hand. So Amnon lay down, and made himself sick: and when the king was come to see him, Amnon said unto the king, I pray thee, let Tamar my sister come, and make me a couple of cakes in my sight, that I may eat at her hand.

Then David sent home to Tamar, saying, Go now to thy brother Amnon's house, and dress him meat. So Tamar went to her brother Amnon's house; and he was laid down. And she took flour, and kneaded it, and made cakes in his sight, and did bake the cakes. And she took a pan, and poured them out before him; but he refused to eat. And Amnon said, Have out all men from me. And they went out every man from him. And Amnon said unto Tamar, Bring the meat into the chamber, that I may eat of thine hand. And

> Tamar took the cakes which she had made, and brought them into the chamber to Amnon her brother. And when she had brought them unto him to eat, he took hold of her, and said unto her, Come lie with me, my sister. And she answered him, Nay, my brother, do not force me; for no such thing ought to be done in Israel: do not thou this folly. And I, whither shall I cause my shame to go? and as for thee, thou shalt be as one of the fools in Israel. Now therefore, I pray thee, speak unto the king; for he will not withhold me from thee. Howbeit he would not hearken unto her voice: but, being stronger than she, forced her, and lay with her. Then Amnon hated her exceedingly; so that the hatred wherewith he hated her was greater than the love wherewith he had loved her.
>
> And Amnon said unto her, Arise, be gone. And she said unto him, There is no cause: this evil in sending me away is greater than the other that thou didst unto me. But he would not hearken unto her. Then he called his servant that ministered unto him, and said, Put now this woman out from me, and bolt the door after her. And she had a garment of divers colours upon her: for with such robes were the king's daughters that were virgins apparelled. Then his servant brought her out, and bolted the door after her. And Tamar put ashes on her head, and rent her garment of divers colours that was on her, and laid her hand on her head, and went on crying.

Amnon didn't just steal his sister's virginity, he stole:
1. Her confidence

2. Her ability to get married
3. Her ability to have children
4. Her reputation
5. Her identity
6. Her voice

Nowadays, as women, we often freely give all of these away. How did he steal all of these gifts from her? Rape is powerful enough to silence most women. While many rapes are reported, most go unreported; this isn't necessarily because the woman fears her attacker. It's oftentimes because she fears the backlash of a society that demands that she remain quiet, especially if her attacker has any measure of influence. Look at the news surrounding R&B sensation, R. Kelly. One of the women who was in "his care" for several years has now broken free, and she's echoing the same sentiments and stories that her predecessors echoed. She said that the Pied Piper of R&B started sleeping with her when she was only 17-years old. She moved in with him when she was 18, and according to her, he forbade her from having a relationship with her family. She also claims that he was abusive, manipulative and sexually sadistic. Again, she's saying what other women have said. She ended up leaving him after he was arrested, and when she saw the Lifetime Series, "Surviving R. Kelly," she realized that she wasn't just his "girlfriend." She realized that everything he'd done to her, he'd done to other women. So, after years of being estranged from her family, she reconciled with them and ended her relationship with her incarcerated lover.

Nevertheless, her character was brutally and mercilessly attacked by thousands upon thousands of his fans, but the most shocking part of it is, the majority (I would venture out to say 80-90%) of the people who harassed the young woman were women! Azriel Clary had been pursuing a music career when she'd met R. Kelly, and he was supposed to help her to establish that career. Howbeit, like the sunglass-wearing demon I'd seen in my dream, he didn't just take something out of her hand, he stole her voice. The Bible tells us that Satan comes to kill, to steal and to destroy. What I've learned about our arch-nemesis is that when he steals a voice, he doesn't silence it. He perverts it. He takes away a woman's confidence in regards to the things of God, but he makes her confident serving him with her abilities (singing abilities, speaking abilities, etc.). Notice, I didn't say voice. He makes her confident in her abilities, but he takes away the relevancy of her voice. Don't get me wrong. Most women can speak and some can sing; Satan's main focus isn't the gift, it's the character behind the gift that he's after. Sure, he'd love to steal all of our gifts, but since the gifts and callings are without repentance, he settles for perverting our minds; this way, he can use our gifts to pervert others. He infuses sex and perversion so much into a woman's soul that she begins to ooze it whenever she speaks, moves and sings. Most women try to take their lives back, but they don't take their voices back, and please understand that speaking out against a predator is only a tenth of what it means to take back your voice.

Sexual Boundaries

Again, Tamar's voice had been stolen. In those days, women who had been raped did better to hide out and remain silent than to accuse their attackers publicly if no one heard them screaming for help. They simply had to remain in their fathers' houses for the rest of their lives, and if no children were born as a result of the attack, they had to remain childless, otherwise, they'd be accused of being whoremongers; society would say it this way, "You played the whore in your father's house." They wouldn't be able to marry because if they did, chances are, the white sheet (purity cloth) would remain white the minute their new husbands attempted to consummate their union together. And if he did not remain silent about this—if he ever decided that he did not want to remain married to the woman, he would use that white sheet to, not only condemn her, but to accuse her father. Consequently, she would be brought outside the door of her father's house and stoned to death by society, so she did better to remain silent and out of view. If her father knew of the rape, chances are, he remained silent as well and simply decided to not give that daughter away in marriage. In other words, it had to remain a secret. This is what King David did. After learning that his son, Amnon, had raped his daughter, Tamar, he did nothing. Tamar hid away in her brother, Absalom's house. According to the scriptures, when she'd left Amnon's room after being raped, she'd ripped her garments. In those days, virgins wore a certain type of garment. She'd entered his room a virgin, but she left bound to a man, albeit, illegally. Let's look at the rest of that story. 2 Samuel 13:18-23 reads, "And she had a garment of

divers colours upon her: for with such robes were the king's daughters that were virgins apparelled. Then his servant brought her out, and bolted the door after her. And Tamar put ashes on her head, and rent her garment of divers colours that was on her, and laid her hand on her head, and went on crying.
And Absalom her brother said unto her, Hath Amnon thy brother been with thee? **But hold now thy peace**, my sister: he is thy brother; regard not this thing. So **Tamar remained desolate in her brother Absalom's house**. But when king David heard of all these things, he was very wroth. And Absalom spake unto his brother Amnon neither good nor bad: for Absalom hated Amnon, because he had forced his sister Tamar."

Tamar remained "desolate" in her brother, Absalom's house. According to Merriam-Webster, the word "desolate" means:
1. devoid of inhabitants and visitors: deserted
2. joyless, disconsolate, and sorrowful through or as if through separation from a loved one
3. showing the effects of abandonment and neglect

What's interesting here is the word "devoid." Ironically enough, when a woman has sex, both inside and outside of the marital covenant, it creates a void. The same is true for men, of course. This is why 1 Corinthians 7:32-34 says, "But I want you to be without care. He who is unmarried cares for the things of the Lord—how he may please the Lord. But he who is married cares about the things of the world—how he may please his wife. There is a difference between a wife and a virgin. The unmarried woman cares about the things of the Lord, that she may be holy both in body and in spirit. But she who is married cares about the things of the world—how she may please her husband." First, notice here that it juxtaposes a wife with a virgin, meaning, biblically speaking, a woman who is not a virgin is seen as married in the eyes of God, but an illegal marriage is called "fornication." This means that the Father did not give her away; this is a contract that was entered into illegally. This doesn't render the contract null and void because the woman agreed! That is, unless, of course, she was forced into marriage. This is to get us to understand what the word "marriage" actually means! The word "marriage" means to be banded together. This is why the groom is called a hus-band! Another word for band is bond. When two come together in sex, they bond their souls (mind, will and emotions) together. When this bond is illegal, it's called bondage. This brings to mind 2 Timothy 3:1-8, which reads, "This know also, that in the last days perilous times shall come. For men shall be lovers of their own selves, covetous, boasters, proud, blasphemers, disobedient to parents, unthankful, unholy, without natural affection, trucebreakers, false accusers, incontinent, fierce, despisers of those that are good, traitors, heady, highminded, lovers of pleasures more than lovers of God; having a form of godliness, but denying the power thereof: from such turn away. **For of this sort are they which creep into houses, and lead captive silly women laden with sins, led away with divers lusts**, ever learning, and never able to come to the knowledge of the truth." Another word for captive or captivity is bondage.

Again, when Satan steals a woman's voice, he doesn't silence it, he perverts it. Let's look at the lyrics of one of the songs (just one) that our youth (and many in the church) are listening to and promoting today! These lyrics are perverting our daughters and teaching them that their bodies are not sacred, but should instead be used for manipulation, control and vindication. Most of the songs out today are from broken women who, in a sense, teach other broken women how to think, behave and survive in a sea of broken men. And there are some songs from broken men who teach other broken men how to seduce, manipulate and mistreat broken women and how to break women. Please note that whenever and wherever you see something blacked out, it's because it was classified as profanity.

Song by Megan, the Stallion

I'm that ▮ (yeah)
Been that ▮, still that ▮ (ah)
Will forever be that ▮ (forever be that ▮)
Yeah (ay, ha)
I'm the hood Mona Lisa, break a n a into pieces
Had to X some cheesy ▮ out my circle like a pizza (yeah)
I'm way too exclusive, I don't shop on Insta' boutiques
All them lil' a clothes only fit fake ▮
Bad ▮, still talking cash ▮

Sexual Boundaries

> ▓▓ like water, I'm unbothered and relaxing
> I would never trip on a ▓▓ if I had him
> ▓▓, that's my trash, you the maid, so you bagged him, ah
> I'm a savage (yeah)
> Classy, bougie, ratchet (yeah)
> Sassy, moody, nasty (hey, hey, yeah)
> Acting stupid, what's happening? ▓▓ (whoa, whoa)
> What's happening? ▓▓ (whoa, whoa)
> I'm a savage, yeah
> Classy, bougie, ratchet, yeah
> Sassy, moody,...

Now, get this. I am not calling her a devil, but she's being used by the devil, just like many of the artists today, but the same could have been said of me had someone handed me a mic and gave me a platform when I was still in my fallen state. In other words, I'm not judging her because I could have easily been her, but the point is, this is exactly what happens when there is no father to protect the daughters or when the fathers have been perverted themselves. What walks out of the door of a home is a direct representative of the father who covers that home, and I'm not talking about Father God. You see, we were born into sin, and this is why we have to be born again. Howbeit, when a woman is used for sex outside of the context of marriage, a void begins to develop in her soul. A void is like a bottomless pit. It has a strong gravitational pull and there's no end to it, plus, there's no way to fill or satisfy it. And get this, because of sin, we all have voids. This is why we have to have fathers or father-figures; this is why we must be covered. The enemy is after our minds, and one way to enter our bodies is through our sexual organs. This is because sex isn't just the coming together of two bodies, it's the merging together of two souls. These souls cannot be broken apart by humans; this is why the scriptures say, "What God has brought together, let no man put asunder." The same is true for relationships that God has not brought together; while they can be "divorced" by man, a soul tie cannot be broken by man. And it is for this reason that more than fifty percent of marriages today end in divorce. Soul ties are similar to the mixing of water. I often use this example to demonstrate my point. If I took water from the Atlantic Ocean and poured it into the Pacific Ocean, the water would become one body. If I decided one day that I wanted to remove the Atlantic Ocean's waters from the Pacific Ocean, I wouldn't be able to designate or distinguish the Atlantic waters from the waters of the Pacific. Consequently, it would be impossible for me to separate these waters. This is what a soul tie looks like. The soul is fluid. When it is mixed with another soul, no divorce decree or restraining order can separate them. As a result, every time a bound woman or a bound man joins themselves to other people, they create a freak. What is a freak? Merriam-Webster defines the word "freak" this way:

1. one that is markedly unusual or abnormal: such as a person or animal having a physical oddity and appearing in a circus sideshow
2. a person who is obsessed with something

When multiple bodies join together, they create a freak show; there are multiple heads and limbs on that body. There is no peace in that body. There are many stomachs in that body, and it is for this reason that every individual in that network finds himself or herself dealing with indecisiveness, instability, rejection, double-mindedness and every other issue underneath the sun. This also creates an unnatural sexual appetite because the voids in each individual are made bigger every time they lie down with someone else. Soon enough, the person starts referring to himself or herself as a "freak," not realizing what he or she is saying. In an attempt to satisfy or silence the cries coming from within that void, the individuals go from one relationship to another, and if the void gets big enough, they start looking at other means to pacify it, including drugs, alcohol, gambling and crime.

In order for a woman to recover her voice and her identity, she has to absolutely and unapologetically create boundaries around her heart. If she protects or guards her heart the way the Bible tells her to, she'll automatically and instinctively guard her body. The same is true for men. But this is easier said than done, especially in a culture that promotes sexual immorality and scoffs at purity. Sexual boundaries are designed to protect your heart! You see, once a woman joins herself to a man illegally, that soul tie creates an appetite that cannot be quenched or satisfied. Sure, she can be in a monogamous relationship (or, at minimum, the appearance of a monogamous relationship), and she can remain faithful to the man she's with, but that void in her will keep on crying out for more. She'll want more hugs, more affirmation, more answers to her many questions and more time. She'll create more problems in her attempt to get more answers. She'll be what the biblical scholars coined a "continual dripping on a very rainy day" (see Proverbs 27:15). This is because a woman who is not content will automatically become contentious. Her void can only be filled by God, and all of our voids aren't just filled one time, contrary to popular belief. We have to dedicate ourselves to God everyday, otherwise, our voids will cry out for more, and we'll look for anything and anyone to fill those empty God-sized holes in our hearts. Ironically enough, I was born with a hole in my heart; to me, this was a prophetic picture of what the first half of my life would look like. Howbeit, when I was nine-years old, I stepped on a nail when we were moving out of our house and into another house. My dad took me to the doctor, and of course, the doctor asked if I had any preexisting conditions. My Dad told him that I had a hole in my heart. The doctor took his stethoscope (I think) and listened to my heart. He said that it sounded normal now, and that the hole had likely filled in. In other words, according to his professional opinion, I was healed. Amazingly enough, the number nine, biblically speaking, represents completeness; it is a symbol of finality.

God's commandments and instructions are more than just mere words, they serve as your hedge of protection. But when you venture outside of them, you'll find yourself being victimized by a villain who's hellbent on stealing your voice, your identity and your future. The question then becomes—how do I create boundaries around myself sexually, especially if I've never seen an example of purity?

1. **You must first want to be pure.** And please understand that sexual purity is more than just refraining from sex; it means to guard your heart. It means to not listen to music that defames God's character and perverts yours! It means to refrain from watching television shows that promote sexual deviancy and immorality. It means to surround yourself with God-fearing people who promote holiness. You have to pray for them and not covet the attention, affirmation or acceptance of the cliques created in Christianity by folks who are still patterning themselves after the world. Understand that a clique is a band, just like a husband is a band. If you fall into the wrong networks, you will find yourself bound, and you'll never be able to go outside of what they consider culturally acceptable.

2. **You have to pursue purity.** This means that you can't be reactive. You have to be proactive. For example, I know that kissing is foreplay for most of us, so I took it off the menu. No man can kiss me except at the altar after the pastor says, "You may now kiss the bride." Surround yourself with pure people, even if you can only find them online. Read books about purity and watch videos that promote purity.

3. **You need examples.** Find couples online and offline who have entered marriage God's way. The setup of

the human soul dictates that we need someone to look up to or an example of what we are to look forward to. Unfortunately, many women don't have positive examples, so they look up to perverted celebrities who pervert them all the more.

4. **Establish Godly boundaries!** When I first launched my business, I had very few rules, and because of this, I endured so much chaos that, like most first-time entrepreneurs, I seriously considered closing my business. I slowly became more and more bitter, and this could be seen under my frequently asked questions tab on my website. In the beginning, I found myself despising women in leadership because women do business different than men. Let me explain. My company tailors to leaders. My male customers, as it would seem, were often nice and easy to work with. Many of my female customers on the other hand, were emotional, indecisive and sometimes even condescending. Not all of them, of course, but I noticed a HUGE difference in transactions I did with men versus the ones I did with women. Women required four times as much time, requested more revisions and rebelled against the posted rules more than men. I soon discovered that this wasn't a woman issue. I'm called to help women. The enemy wanted to pervert my view of my sisters; this way, I would become ineffective as a leader. Eventually, I obeyed God and started not only establishing rules (boundaries), I started religiously

enforcing them. When I did this, my customer-base seemed to dwindle. Business seemed to slow down to almost a complete halt for a season, and even though I oftentimes wondered if I'd done the right thing, something in me wouldn't let me be passive about what I was building. Slowly, but surely, business began to pick up all the more, and before I knew it, I was making more money and working with a better quality of customers. When I say "quality," I mean in reference to mindsets. I started having both stable male and female customers because my boundaries and prices scared away the unstable ones. That year, my profits more than doubled! And every year after that, my profits seemed to either double or nearly double. I learned how valuable boundaries are, but it is to be noted that when you establish them, there is a season of loneliness and quietness as you transition from one mindset to another. This is the wilderness season. It is a space between the perversion and the promise. Most believers return to their perversion while in this season because they get tired of waiting on God to bring them into the promise, so they settle for anything and anyone who's willing to serve as a void-filler. One way to establish Godly boundaries is to create a menu. On this menu, list the allowances and restrictions of a man or woman who's pursuing a relationship with you. For example, "He can call me everyday, but I don't take calls after 11 pm. He cannot come to my house, nor will I go to his house. We will not be alone together. No kissing before marriage. No foreplay or fooling around. He must be saved, sanctified and filled with the Holy Spirit. He must have a church home and be submitted to a leader." These are what we called "standards," and believe it or not, a standard is a boundary. The goal of a boundary is to show you who's bound because bound people do not like, nor will they honor boundaries! This is what God meant when He said to test the spirits! Create a menu of boundaries and submit it to your leader or mentor. Ask the leader to tell you what's reasonable versus what's unreasonable and unrealistic. Allow the leader to add or remove items from your menu unless, of course, they are removing something you personally feel like you need. For example, a leader with relaxed standards (doesn't mean they're bad, just means they aren't very strict) may scratch off the "no kissing before marriage" rule, citing that they kissed their spouses before marriage and nothing happened. Howbeit, they may not have struggled with the demons you've struggled with. If lust, rape, molestation, promiscuity and sexual immorality is in your past, you may need to keep the no-kissing clause on your menu. As a matter of fact, I admonish you to keep it there! For example, kissing for most of us makes us want to have sex! This is especially true when we go from normal kissing to French kissing. From there, it is difficult to abstain; in truth, it's nearly impossible to abstain for most of us! This is why God told us to flee fornication. This means that you don't walk away, you have to literally take off running the same way that Joseph ran when Potiphar's wife grabbed him and said, "Lie with me." Joseph wasn't running from the woman, he was running from himself! He knew that if he stood there and tried to resist, he would slowly begin to relax his standards as his blood rushed to his "other member." He didn't think about it or talk about it. He just ran! Now, imagine if he'd reasoned within himself that he'd just kiss her for a few seconds and leave. Potiphar's wife would have become Joseph's concubine in the twinkling of an eye! From there, her soul would have been divided, her loyalties would have been divided and her mind would have slowly begun to split; this is when she would have started saying things like, "I'm confused. Potiphar treats me well, but when I'm with Joseph, he makes me feel like gravity doesn't exist! I'm madly in love with him, but I don't want to lose Potiphar either!" This is the conversation of a double-minded and unstable individual who is under the influence of another human being!

5. **Enforce your boundaries!** Every time you establish a boundary, Satan will send someone to test that boundary. For example, when I first started establishing boundaries in business, I had people who tested them by saying things like, "I can't give you a deposit. I'm sorry. I refuse to pay for something I haven't seen" or "I understand you said that I get one

free revision, but there's no way I'm paying for a second revision!" There were times when I removed the boundaries and there were times when I relaxed the boundaries, and I dare to say this—in 99.9% of the cases when I didn't honor my own established boundaries, what first appeared to be a normal and friendly customer and a problem-free transaction turned into chaos. Most of the times when I lifted a boundary, it was because the customer was extremely kind, patient, and in some cases, generous. I felt that I could make the exception for them for those reasons, but the minute I lifted those boundaries, things took a dark turn. It was as if God was having to repeatedly teach me the same lesson until I learned to not be transactional in my thinking. In other words, I had to learn that someone being extremely nice and accommodating did not have to be followed up with rewards, after all, it was that mode of reasoning that led and kept me in fornication for so many years. One of the hardest lessons I've ever had to learn was how to receive a blessing without feeling like I needed to reciprocate that blessing in one way or another. This is true for most women because, culturally speaking, society teaches us (through mediums like music and movies) that every good deed should be rewarded, and then, it promotes sex as a reasonable reward; this is transactional thinking. For example, you'll notice that most "love scenes" in a movie were preceded by a kind gesture. In the movie Soul Food,

Sexual Boundaries

Miles is a married man who ends up having an adulterous affair with Faith, his wife's cousin; this had been preceded by Faith's attentiveness and support of Miles' musical craft, and Miles' support and help with Faith's career in dance. This is a theme in many of today's movies. It promotes the idea that sex is a justifiable means by which a kind act or gesture should be rewarded. Consequently, most broken and/or immature men and women use it as a means of currency. Again, when you establish a boundary, you have to be willing to enforce it at all costs! Most women and men relax their boundaries when their insignificant others do something nice for them, especially if it is slowly becoming a trend. They don't know how to respond to kind gestures, so they exchange sexual favors for love, time, peace and validation. This is prostitution, no matter how we look at it! One of the most difficult things to do, especially if you have a lot of rejection and sexual immorality in your background, is to learn not to necessarily reciprocate kind deeds, but to just say "thank you" and then override the temptation to do something in return. This takes intentionality, accountability and planning! This takes prayer! And know that whenever you start enforcing boundaries, people will leave your life. God said in James 4:7, "Submit yourselves therefore to God. Resist the devil, and he will flee from you." This means that any time you resist the devil's advances, he will flee from you. All the same, his children will run as well.

6. **Defend your boundaries!** One lesson I've learned is that not all Christians have the same standards. When you have standards, lines and borders that most Christians don't have, they'll label you as "religious." The word "religious" is often used to condescend someone who, quite frankly, has separated himself or herself from the world in such a way that the person has truly become authentic. In the Christian realm, an authentic person is equivalent to what the secular realm would label as a nerd. Nerds aren't always openly accepted by their peers, even though their work and work ethic are often celebrated and promoted to encourage others to strive for better. One of the hardest things I've ever had to do was to defend my boundaries, for example, I don't listen to secular music, especially music that promotes sex, violence, pride or sin. When I got saved, I honestly thought this was the standard for most Christians. So, getting rid of my music playlist was a real challenge for me. I actually cried about it, prayed about it, tried to reason with God about it, etc. It took a lot of prayer and consecration for me to turn away from music that told me that I was a good for nothing whore who only had value in a relationship (this is what most music promotes today, even though most people won't admit this). When I started coming around believers, I was honestly shocked to see what they were into. Seriously! I saw women twerking and

gossiping; I saw men lusting after women, lusting after other men and chasing after everything but God. I was taken aback! Nevertheless, I held my stance, and to my surprise, I had to watch people passively insinuate that I was religious. I honestly started to believe that most Christians see my stance as an immature one; they think that as I grow into my wings, I'll eventually embrace twerking and reveling again. Even though I've matured in Christ long ago, many people who've been "saved" longer than I have reason that any woman who is uncomfortable being carnal is just afraid; they reason that she's wounded, immature and misguided. It's a lie. I will never return to the vomit God delivered me from because that's the level of consecration that God has called me to, plus, I'm grateful that He saw fit to deliver me from that the music, the moves and all that I once treasured in the world. Instead, they were placed on an altar I created in my heart for Him and sacrificed! I will never resurrect it just to fit in! This brings me to the next pointer.

7. **Promote your boundaries—out loud!** The consensus is that silence gives consent. Silence is complicity! As in the days of old, you can never allow the pressures of society to weigh you down so much that you favor fitting in over promoting holiness. So, if your boundaries were established by God, promote them, but don't beat people up with them. In other words, don't use them to make people feel bad about

being complicit. When I was immature, I was very abrasive because I was mad at most "church folks" for being so carnal. But I soon realized that I was no better. I'd just been intentional about slaying my dragons, but this is because I didn't grow up in a traditional church setting. Again, I'd left the church at the age of eight, so even though I understood the religious movements, shenanigans and phrases that were prevalent in many Christian churches, I didn't understand the true heart of God. But as I died to myself, I continued to promote my boundaries, but in a more loving way. I also stopped being apologetic for my stance, after all, I have no desire to "fit in." I just want to be who I'm designed to be. This is the stance or the attitude that every believer who wants to live a life that's pleasing to God, not just in works, but in heart, must take.

8. **Revisit and re-establish your boundaries.** A kingdom didn't just have boundaries surrounding the land they owned, they looked to increase those boundaries.. so they traded with other nations, went to war with other nations and bought more property. This is called expansion. Every believer should be looking to expand. But Kingdom expansion isn't the by-product of working hard, it is the by-product of faith coupled with works. In every given season, you'll learn more about what you can do, what you shouldn't do and what you should not be a part of. Remember, your level of consecration may not look like everybody

else's, especially if God has called you to the forefront. For example, I got delivered from fornication while married. I remember standing to my feet and shouting out to God, "I repent!" These words weren't just words to me. I sincerely meant them with everything in me. As time progressed, I found myself feeling like it wasn't enough. Now, don't get me wrong—when I say that it wasn't enough, I'm not talking about having to buy my salvation or to purchase God's favor. I'm talking about what I needed to become the woman God designed me to be. Before long, I found myself creating another boundary. I shouted, "Lord, if I'm ever single again, I won't even kiss a man before marriage!" What was I doing? I was revisiting and reestablishing my boundaries. Note: if you start relaxing your boundaries, you run the risk of falling into temptation.

Remember, sexual boundaries must be established in your mind. You first have to understand why God is against sex outside of marriage; this allows you to come into agreement with Him. And if you're unsure, remember that God created sex for married couples to enjoy. Sex was designed for reproduction, intimacy and to tighten the connection between a husband and wife. It also serves as a stress reliever. Oregon Health and Science University reported the following health benefits that sex provides for women alone:
- Lower blood pressure
- Better immune system

- Better heart health, possibly including lower risk for heart disease
- Improved self-esteem
- Decreased depression and anxiety
- Increased libido
- Immediate, natural pain relief
- Better sleep
- Increased intimacy and closeness to a sexual partner
- Overall stress reduction, both physiologically and emotional

Amazingly enough, stress does the exact opposite to the body and much more! Everything that God created has benefits whenever it's utilized within the boundaries of His will, but when it's taken advantage of outside of His will, it produces chaos. Consider Proverbs 10:22, which reads, "The blessing of the LORD makes rich, and he adds no sorrow with it." Please note that the word "ploutos" is the Greek word for "rich" and according to Strong's Concordance, it literally means "wealth, abundance, materially or spiritually." In other words, when God's blessing is on a system, God then builds a shield around it to protect the integrity, functionality and the health of that system. This also means that anything acquired outside of His will is not covered, empowered or protected by Him. This means that it is accursed! Sex outside of the context of marriage is accursed; there's no way around this. Webster's Revised Unabridged Dictionary defines the word "accursed" as "under a curse; doomed to evil or misery; ill-fated." Of course, if the word "bless" means "empowered to prosper," the word "curse" or "accursed" means "something that is rejected or something that is designed to fail." This is why the narcissist needs the sin offering. Satan wants to remove God from any and everything that we build or establish; this way, he can have legal rights to it. Howbeit, when we do as Romans 12:1 instructed and that is to present our bodies as living sacrifices, holy and acceptable to God, which is our reasonable service, we'll reap the benefits of healthy, God-approved marriages that the enemy can't touch!

FINANCIAL BOUNDARIES

1 Kings 17:1-9: And Elijah the Tishbite, who was of the inhabitants of Gilead, said unto Ahab, As the LORD God of Israel liveth, before whom I stand, there shall not be dew nor rain these years, but according to my word. And the word of the LORD came unto him, saying, Get thee hence, and turn thee eastward, and hide thyself by the brook Cherith, that is before Jordan. And it shall be, that thou shalt drink of the brook; and I have commanded the ravens to feed thee there. So he went and did according unto the word of the LORD: for he went and dwelt by the brook Cherith, that is before Jordan. And the ravens brought him bread and flesh in the morning, and bread and flesh in the evening; and he drank of the brook. And it came to pass after a while, that the brook dried up, because there had been no rain in the land. And the word of the LORD came unto him, saying, Arise, get thee to Zarephath, which belongeth to Zidon, and dwell there: behold, I have commanded a widow woman there to sustain thee.

In the above story, we meet a prophet by the name of Elijah. Elijah had just made a prophetic declaration over Gilead, stating that there would be no rain in the land for several years because of Jezebel and Ahab's idolatrous and murderous ways. After this, God told him to hide himself by the brook Cherith, and from there, God told the ravens to feed the prophet. Of course, they did as they were told. Nevertheless, at some point, the brook began to dry up. Was this a surprise to God? No. He'd honored the word of the Prophet Elijah and He'd shut up Heaven on his behalf. So, when the brook dried up, God told Elijah to arise. The word "arise" comes from the Greek word "egeirō" and it means to come from a lower place or a position to a higher one. What God was essentially telling the prophet to do was to come out of his comfort zone. Now, I want you to imagine what life would have been like had Elijah refused to move. Imagine him shouting into the air, "I'm waiting on God! He will supply all of my needs!" Please note that experts say that we can live up to a week without water; for some, that number is a measly three days. Within a few days, Elijah would have started suffering from the effects of dehydration, some of which include:

- Unquenchable thirst
- Dry or sticky mouth
- Inability to urinate
- Dizziness
- Dark urination
- Painful urination
- Headache
- Muscle cramps
- Dry skin
- Rapid heartbeat
- Rapid breathing
- Lethargy
- Hallucinations

In the midst of these symptoms, he would have found himself fainting and slowly losing consciousness until he finally gave up the ghost. The brook represented the voice of God, since water is symbolic of the Word. Elijah had to follow the voice of God. Had he not done so, he would have suffered an even greater drought; that is, he would have been a prophet who could not hear the voice of God. This is what happened to Abram when he took Lot with him on a journey that God clearly told him to take alone. Genesis 12:1 reads, "Now the LORD had said unto Abram, Get thee out of thy country, and <u>from thy kindred</u>, and from thy father's house, unto a land that I will shew thee." Genesis 12:4 details the start of Abram's journey. It states, "So Abram departed, as the LORD had spoken unto him; and <u>Lot went with him</u>: and Abram was seventy and five years old when he departed out of Haran." If you'll continue reading Genesis 12 and Genesis 13, you'll notice that God did not speak to Abram until he parted ways with Lot. Genesis 13:14 reads, "And the LORD said unto Abram, <u>after that Lot was separated from him</u>, Lift up now thine eyes, and look from the place where thou art northward, and southward, and eastward, and westward." Anytime a prophet disobeys God, that prophet runs the risk of shutting off God's mic in his or her life. And we see this a lot today. A lot of prophets are enduring God-droughts because they've chosen to live outside of God's will. The same is true for us. Whenever you stop hearing the voice of God, this may signal that it's time for you to move. To move isn't necessarily a physical act; you may or may not have to move out of your house or out of your state. God may be calling you to move on from a relationship, to change your mind about a person or to move past an offense. But whenever you refuse to move, like Elijah, you run the risk of dealing with a financial drought. What many believers do not know or understand is this—God's grace covers you when you venture past the boundary of God's will, but if you stay outside of His will, He is not obligated to finance your stay there.

The year was 2007 and I was in the middle of a divorce. I was a babe in Christ, meaning, I was immature or, better yet, I lacked knowledge. I'd been separated from my estranged husband for around six to nine months and winter was quickly approaching. I lived alone in a huge home and I'd been trying to weather the effects of the divorce on my own, save a close friend of mine. Before long, news got out about my separation (I'd managed to keep it private), and not long after that, I found myself being surrounded by people (this was what I'd been trying to avoid the whole time). I made a lot of new friends and a few estranged kin-folks of mine even started reappearing in my life. "You've been single long enough! It's time for you to start dating again!" I remember one of my new friends saying this to me. I knew it wasn't right, even though I was still relatively immature in the faith. Nevertheless, having a romantic prospect in my life didn't sound like such a bad idea. At first, I resisted, but one day, my friend decided to take it upon herself to introduce me to a guy. She told me about this dark, handsome guy that every woman in town wanted to get with, but he hadn't had any success in getting a good woman. I remember what she said to me. "He looks just like Morris Chestnut!" Immediately, I thought of an ex of mine; somehow, I knew who she was talking about. When she said his name, I sat up on my couch, crossed my arms and looked at her. As it turned out, the guy was an ex of mine; I'd dated him for about a year when I was 16-years old and again, when I was around 20-years old, and in truth, we'd broken up both times because he'd cheated. He was an extremely handsome, soft-spoken, but broken guy. When I told her that he was an ex of mine, she insisted that he was a changed man and that I should, at minimum, talk with him. I reluctantly agreed, but I pretty much told her that the man I was divorcing was a nun in comparison to that guy. I remember telling her that it was the same devil in a different dude. Howbeit, I gave her permission to give him my number.

This particular ex was someone who, even after we'd broken up, had remained close with my family. As a matter of fact, before I'd met and married the man I was in the process of divorcing, we'd tried two or three times to restart our relationship over the years, but it had failed each time because he was promiscuous. But let's fast-forward; she gave him my number and when he called me, I was ready for his romantic antics. I knew that he was convinced that I was "the one," but this didn't mean that I would be the only one. I considered how handsome he was, but I couldn't get past the fact that he did not and would not know how to be faithful to a woman. We talked over the phone, and he asked

Financial Boundaries

if he could come and see me—at my house—at the house I'd shared with my ex-husband. My resounding "no" sounded like a resounding "yes" to him. He assured me that he'd respect my boundaries and that we would just talk. Before long, I found myself relaxing my boundaries and saying yes. "But you have to park in the garage," I said. "Because my ex-husband likes to drive by this house, and if he sees your car in the driveway, he's gonna torch this house with the both of us in it." He laughed, but he agreed, after all, he had played the side-dude before with women.

A day or two later, he pulled up in my driveway and I used the remote to let up the garage. I remember his dilapidated car pulling into the garage; it was a loud eyesore, and to be honest with you, it almost felt like confirmation that he wasn't the guy for me. There was no way I was going to reconcile with that guy, not because of his car, but because he just didn't have his life together in any area. His greatest quality at that time was his looks and physique. To me, at best, he'd end up being some rich woman's handsome pool-boy-slash-boy-toy because while he did look nice to the eyes, he wasn't at all ambitious. He came into the house and we started talking. I knew the right questions to ask him, after all, I was around 30-years old, so I'd known the guy for 14 years. After all the small-talk was over, I went straight to the point. "Who's the woman in your life?" I asked, staring him directly in his eyes. He hesitated. I could tell that he didn't want to answer, but by then, he knew that I would find out within a few days to a week. That had been our history. He dropped his head and started fumbling with his fingers. Finally, he said her name. I didn't know her, but I knew him. I knew that there was a "her" somewhere, and I wanted to go ahead and disqualify him before my friend got too excited about the prospect of he and I getting back together. "But she's in the military," he said. "Full-time, so I haven't seen her for about six months." A wave of relief hit me. Because, even though I knew there was no way he and I could be together past a week or two (that's how long it normally took me to catch him), I had been entertaining the oh-so-infamous "what if" thoughts, plus, my friend had been so excited about "us", especially after learning that we had an extensive history together. She was absolutely convinced that he was "the one" and that it was God Himself bringing us back together. "Girl, I know it's God because every time I see you, I think of him!" she would passionately reiterate every time we talked about him. But as he sat there on my couch, I knew that I'd made another mistake; I'd given him my phone number, my address and I'd let him in my house. We talked about his new girl, my failed marriage and our individual plans for the future. After he'd reluctantly told me that he had a girlfriend, he knew that there was no way he and I were going to reconcile, even though he said a few times, "I think I'm going to break up with her." I wasn't impressed and I didn't hide it. Instead our "date" turned into a fuss session, with me telling him that he needed to settle down and stop slinging his butt all around town. Not long after that, I waved as he backed out of my driveway with his car's engine making it darn near impossible for us to hear anything. I couldn't wait to tell my friend that he was a no-go so she could stop talking about him. This young lady was in the world, and in truth, she was very prophetic (she was the first person who said to the adult-sized me that God was going to use me, and that I would be a household name). Howbeit, with him, she'd missed the mark. Not long after that, I did end up getting myself a boyfriend, and as it would turn out, he was also going through a divorce, so we were both in adultery. I'd let this guy come to my house, and for about two months, we didn't touch each other. He'd sleep on one end of my couch, and I'd sleep on the other whenever he came to visit. I thought that my abstinence journey was going to be a super-successful one because I'd clearly articulated my boundaries to the guy, and he'd agreed to honor them. All the same, he hadn't touched me, not even so much to kiss me. But one day, that all changed.

"William" and I were watching a horror movie one day, and like always, he was sitting on one end of my sectional, while I was on the other end. The sectional was huge because my den was massive in size. I'd cooked and we'd just finished eating while watching the movie. After that, I grabbed a blanket and proceeded to scream and cover my head every time something would jump out in the movie. That's when I heard William's voice. He said something to the effect of, "I hate to see you like that. Sometimes, I want to hold you, but you won't let me. I know that you're a woman of God. I, too, am a man of God. Just sit next to me. I just want to hold and protect you." Being held sounded so good in that hour.

Slowly, but surely, I stood to my feet and made my way towards another boundary. I stepped across that boundary and sat next to William. He pulled the cover over me and wrapped his arms around me. In that moment, I felt safe, wanted and loved. He tightened his grip on me the minute I jumped, and we proceeded to watch the movie. Well, at least, he did. Once I'd crossed that boundary and sat next to him, I'd started focusing on that ever-so-seductive cologne he was wearing, the warmth of his body and the sound of his heart. That's when he crossed a boundary that I'd clearly relaxed. He squeezed me in his arms all the more, leaned over and kissed me on the forehead. That was it. My abstinence became a history lesson on that day.

After that, I felt terrible because, even though I was a babe in Christ, I genuinely desired to honor and please God. I told William that we'd made a mistake and that it couldn't happen again. ~~It wouldn't happen again~~. While the word "no" is a boundary, it has little to no power if other boundaries are not established and enforced to solidify it. In other words, if I was going to keep allowing him in my home, my no would be nothing but a yes wearing a costume. Once he undressed my no, my clothes would follow suit. It couldn't happen again. ~~It wouldn't happen again~~. But it did. And every time we fell, I would end up feeling horrible, put him out of my house and have that same, "I'm a woman of God" conversation with him. Finally, I realized that it wasn't working. If I let him in my house, we were going to keep crossing that boundary until I no longer felt guilty about it, so I told William that he could no longer come to my house. What was I doing? I was establishing another boundary, but I didn't fully enforce it at first. William didn't agree with my stance. "No, we'll go back to sitting far apart," he'd countered. But I wasn't having it because we'd tried our own version of in-house social distancing before, and we'd failed each time. Nevertheless, he showed up at my house a few times, and two or three occasions, I'd made the mistake of opening the door and trying to command my boundaries. He'd come into the house and slowly, but surely, my boundaries would relax, and I'd end up crying out to God, apologizing for my behavior once he left the next day. The last time he'd come to my house, I knew that I had to do something different if I wanted a different result. I had a small window on my door and I utilized it to communicate with him. "No!" I shouted staring at him through that small window pane. "I told you that you couldn't come over here! Why are you here?! Are you three shades of crazy?!" William tried everything to get me to open that door, including claiming that he so desperately needed to use the bathroom. I didn't fall for it. "There's a gas station up the street!" I said. "Or you can go pee in my backyard, but you're not coming in here." Finally, I was enforcing my newfound boundaries. A few minutes later, William said what I needed to hear. "Ma'am, you can't start having sex with a man and just stop! It doesn't work like that! I'm addicted to you, so you can't just stop cold-turkey!" I closed the blinds and walked away. "I'm not opening this door! Call me when you leave," I said, knowing what I needed to do. When William finally left and called me, I ended our relationship. It had become painfully clear to me that our relationship had been ordained in hell because he could not and would not respect my boundaries. Of course, he didn't take the news well, nor did he want to honor my wishes, so I just stopped taking his calls altogether. But what amazed me is this—the minute I allowed William in my house, even though we weren't sexually active at that time, my finances had dried up. It was as if a vacuum cleaner hose had been attached to my bank account and was sucking the life out of every dollar I earned. I almost felt like my bank account had been, at that time, a hospice center for money. Not long after that, I lost that house to foreclosure. But God's grace was still sufficient for me. I hadn't realized that the house had been foreclosed on when an agent entered it while I was at work. Thankfully, he'd seen my pictures in the house and had said to himself, "This is a sister" (he was a Black man). He then went out of his way to find out my name and contact me. His investigation led him to my mother's house. He told her that the bank had foreclosed on my house, and because of this, everything I owned in that house was now the property of the bank. But he didn't want me to lose my stuff, so he was going to put the job off (this was on a Thursday) until Monday; this would give me the weekend to collect my belongings. When I met him, he said to me that when he'd seen my pictures in the house, he'd uttered these words, "Oh man, that's a sister! I can't do her like that!" He went on to tell me that if the bank had sent someone else, they would have legally locked me out and there was nothing I could have done. They would have hired some people to clean out the house, but they would not have allowed me to get my things. Those people would have thrown away some stuff, but kept whatever they wanted to keep. Please note that my house was huge and filled with furniture and expensive things. I even collected wine at that time; I had over one hundred bottles of wine! I knew this was God protecting me in His own unique way. I could sense God's presence all over that guy, so I thanked him and called a few people to help me move my things into storage.

Why did I tell this story? It's simple. My brook had dried up because I hadn't honored the boundaries God had given me. For one, I was still married. My divorce hadn't been finalized yet. William was still married. His divorce hadn't been finalized yet. Next, even if we had both been completely single and available, I should not have allowed him in my house! Now, this truth isn't a popular one because most Christians will argue that they can allow their romantic interests in their homes, but just exercise a few precautionary measures to ensure that they don't fall into the lap of fornication. But what does the Word say?
- "Abstain from all appearance of evil" (Thessalonians 5:22).
- "Watch and pray so that you will not fall into temptation. The spirit is willing, but the flesh is weak" (Matthew 26:41/NIV).
- "When the devil had finished all this tempting, he left him <u>until an opportune time</u>" (Luke 4:13/NIV).
- "No temptation has overtaken you that is not common

to man. God is faithful, and he will not let you be tempted beyond your ability, but with the temptation he will also provide the <u>way of escape</u>, that you may be able to endure it" (1 Corinthians 10:13/ESV).
- "Let not then your good be evil spoken of" (Romans 14:16).

What's both crazy and amazing to me is that I did things in reverse. I fell, and then, I started establishing and enforcing the boundaries I should have set the first time.
- I refused to allow William back in my house.
- I ended my sexual relationship with William.
- I ended a romantic relationship that should have never started in the first place.
- I stopped taking William's calls.
- I repented.

But this wasn't enough, and I'm thankful that it wasn't. You see, God knew that I still had a heart of fornication. I didn't know exactly why it was wrong; I just knew that God said not to do it. So, He knew that if I'd kept that house, I would have fallen into temptation again, so the way of escape He'd created for me was called foreclosure. I lost my house and moved in with the friend who'd passionately and repeatedly rebuked me for having William over in the first place. This friend was Christian and she'd agreed to be my accountability partner.

What I learned is that financial boundaries clearly border

sexual boundaries. I think about the time when I had two Siberian Huskies. I'd had my male for two years and my female for a few months. The goal was to breed the two of them because there weren't many Siberian Huskies in my city. In truth, most people thought they were wolves (my male was part wolf). When the female turned six-months old, she'd gone into heat. She wasn't fully grown, so I didn't want to breed her, but my ex (we were still married then) didn't see anything wrong with breeding them. I took to the internet to see what the experts said, and I came across a site for Huskies. I reached out to the site's owner and she responded almost immediately. She was clearly passionate about dogs and I could see this in her email. She told me that my dog was too young to breed, and if we bred her at that time, it would stunt her growth, plus, this would put her puppies at risk. I was relieved. She was still a puppy and I didn't want her being bred. My ex read the email and he finally agreed. We'd wait until she was at least a year old. So, we had to take on the arduous task of keeping the two dogs separated. I didn't realize how much damage a male dog would do when he smelled a female in heat. That dog broke two windows, clawed up a door (beyond repair) and nearly destroyed an entire room trying to get out to her. We'd created boundaries around her, and he was in no way ready or willing to accept those boundaries. We successfully kept them apart, but we had to replace two windows, a door and a lot of furniture.

Breeding her would have stunted her growth. Those words

never escaped me. They would echo in my mind for years on end. They remind me of the Song of Solomon 8:4 (CSB), which reads, "Young women of Jerusalem, I charge you, do not stir up or awaken love until the appropriate time." Please understand that, as humans, we:
1. Grow up in the flesh.
2. Mature in the spirit.

The words "adult" and "mature" are not synonymous with one another. This is why there are a lot of grown children raising children. This is also why there are so many generational curses and not enough "good men" and "good women" leaving an inheritance for their children and their children's children.

Every human is like a country; we are all divided up into territories. We all have:

Governor	Love/Law	Overall Ruler
Eros	Romantic Love	Your Choice
Storge	Familial Love	Your Choice

Philia	Brotherly Love	Your Choice
Agape	God's Love/Unconditional	Your Choice

States/Regions of Thought	Interpretation	State/Governor
Mentality	State of Mind	All
• Livelihood	Hood or Neighborhood of Thinking Regarding Money	All
Physicality	State of Being	All
Spirituality	State of Faith	Agape
• Religiosity or Piety	State of Religion	Agape/State of Mind
Familiarity	Familial State	Storge
• Parenthood	Hood or Neighborhood of Thinking Regarding Parenting	Storge/Hood or Neighborhood of Thinking
• Brotherhood/ Sisterhood	Hood or Neighborhood of Thinking Regarding Friendship	Philia/Hood or Neighborhood of Thinking
• Romanticism	Hood or Neighborhood of Thinking Regarding Romance	Eros/Hood or Neighborhood of Thinking

• Sexuality	Hood or Neighborhood of Thinking Regarding Sex	Eros/State of Mind

Note: Sexuality should be a city and fall under Romanticism, and of course, how we relate to one another romantically is directly tied to our relationship with God. Some people have opted to make their sexuality an independent state, meaning, it is no longer tied to their relationship with God, nor is it tied to their romantic state.

Every state is governed by love, but should be ruled by the Word of God. Nevertheless, we get to elect the Presidents for each state. And each of these states has laws, allowances, restrictions and borders. All the same, each of these states has cities, and each city has a mind; the mind of each city is the mayor of that city. For example, our financial state can be broken up into the following cities:
- Tithing
- Giving/Sowing/Investing
- Earning
- Spending

Again, each of these cities is run by a mayor. Of course, you are the mayor of each city; that is, if you haven't given up your seat or relinquished your authority in that area. Each state has neighborhoods, and each state borders another state. This means that whatever I allow in my sexual state can easily cross over into my financial state; this is called advancement. This is what enemies or foreign territories would do in times of war. They would cross a boundary, entering the territory of their enemies. They would then began to fight against their enemies, and if they prevailed, they would drive them further and further back as they staked claim to their territories. But to get into each of our states, the enemy must first enter through the conscious mind and eventually make his way through the subconscious mind. Once he gets into the subconscious, he begins to burrow or dig. This is how he advances toward each state of being and state of mind. When a city or a state is in ruins, the official of that place calls for a state of emergency. Believe it or not, a lot of Christians live in a repeated state of emergency, which is why they make so many bad decisions.

Each city and state has a court system; they are:
1. The conscious mind
2. The subconscious mind
3. The unconscious mind

Again, the conscious mind is pretty much the waiting room of your subconscious. It deals with what's presently engaging your mind at any time, for example, if a man approached you spewing a bunch of false doctrinal gibberish, he would be engaging your conscious mind. In other words, you may not necessarily believe what he's saying, but he has your attention. The information he shares with you will go and sit in your conscious mind unless, that is, you immediately reject it, calling it false. This is what we call a seed. This is what Jesus was talking about in Matthew 18:18. He said, "Verily I say unto you, Whatsoever ye shall bind on earth shall be bound in heaven: and whatsoever ye shall loose on earth shall be loosed in heaven." In other words, whatever you allow or give permission to in your life, Heaven has to allow it as well, but whatever you forbid, Heaven will forbid. Again, you are the governor and the mayor of each city and state of you.

The subconscious mind is where your heart lies; it's the place that God told you to guard. This is where your belief system is stored. This is the heart of your decisions. It's the place that Satan covets the most. He knows that if he can hijack your belief system, he can derail your life. He'd have the remote control to every given city and state. So, when God said for us to guard our hearts, He was dealing with our subconscious minds. He is telling us to be mindful of what we allow to enter into our ear-gates and our eye-gates, and what we allow to escape our mouths. There are many apostles, prophets, pastors, evangelists and teachers locked away in psyche wards because they neglected to guard their hearts. The same is true about graveyards. There are so many people who were called to the five-fold ministry who lost their lives prematurely because they did not guard their hearts. Consequently, Satan went through each state of their being, devouring up everything that was of importance to them. He got them to relax their standards more and more until they finally became cities without walls. From there, he continued to advance on each state, sabotaging and destroying everything in his path. Before long, these would-be leaders found themselves not knowing the difference between what's real versus what's not real. Some of them became super religious, paranoid and fearful. Then again, some of these people aren't in asylums; they are on Instagram Live somewhere wearing a tallit on their heads and shouting at the viewers.

Your financial state is another one of those states that Satan passionately desires to enter. This is because, if he can control your finances, he can essentially control your decisions. For example, a lot of believing women aren't ambitious at all. Don't get me wrong; they want to have money. Some of them even dream of being wealthy, but they aren't willing to put in the time, the effort or make the necessary sacrifices to reach this place, so they sit around and decorate themselves, waiting for some unsuspecting guy to come along and make their lives better. But while waiting on these guys to magically appear, they have to deal with those reoccurring events called bills that we all have to deal with. They live paycheck-to-paycheck, and they can't afford to do many of the things that most of us enjoy doing like traveling, going out to eat or going to some events. And then, they meet a man. What's amazing is the fact that these guys have jobs and they're making three dollars an hour more than what the women are making, plus, these guys work full time. Because their financial states are governed by lust (an ungodly desire), the enemy is able to cross over from that state into their romantic state. This causes them to become transactional in their thinking, meaning, every time a man does something nice for them, they feel the need to repay him somehow. After all, he's doing things for them that they have not and will not do for themselves, since most of their money goes toward decorating themselves. Before long, Satan is able to hijack their imaginations; this is the television in the room of the conscious mind. Of course, they don't do like God tells us to do and that is to cast down those imaginations. In other words, change the channel. They start daydreaming of spending the rest of their lives with their beaus, having children with these guys and what it would be like to sleep with these guys. As Satan plays around in their imaginations, he slowly crosses the romantic border and enters their sexual states. Before long, they find themselves laid across somebody's bed, trying to consummate with the imagination or the advertisement that Satan showed them. They keep this up until the guilt subsides. They no longer feel guilty about being in sexual immorality, but instead, they take a stance against holiness and anyone who preaches it. What they don't realize is that they are transactional; they are trying to pay for love using sex as a means of currency. This is prostitution, and it only serves to damage their financial states all the more. This is why so many women today have two or more children, and they have to rely on the government to support those children. When this happens, the enemy leads them further and further into idolatry, meaning, he removes God as the head of their financial states; those states then start being governed by lust or demand. They now have to feed their children. They have to have a roof over their heads. And because they enter "survival mode," it's a lot easier for them to leave the borders down in their romantic and sexual states because of the condition of their financial states. This means that they are constantly holding an election, choosing which god to serve on any given day. If the enemy gets the best of them financially, it's easy for them to be governed by their needs or their children's needs, and while God is still the President in their lives, they are directly serving Mammon and Poverty. And to my beautiful sisters, if this is you, don't get offended. Just be informed about how the enemy has been seducing you into poverty; this way, you can come out of it and tap into God's love and will for you. The point is, every boundary borders another state; every decision we make affects other decisions. This is also why a needy person cannot be trusted. That person is in a state of emergency and will likely do just about anything to come out of that state.

Another financial boundary includes sowing into bad ground. One example I like to give is this—consider the story of Elijah. The brook dried up. If God wanted to keep him in Gilead, He would have caused water to come out of a rock or He would have found some way to supply the prophet with water. He wanted Elijah to go to Zarephath. If one of the birds that God had commanded to feed Elijah had continued to feed him or had supplied him with water outside of God's will, that bird would have paid a heavy price for its decisions.

Let's look at this example in modern-day terms. A relative of yours is in fornication. God wants her to come out of it, but she refuses. She's Christian, but she is in rebellion. The Bible says that rebellion is as the sin of witchcraft, meaning, it involves a power that is contrary to the power of God. To get her out of this sin, God stops supplying her while she's there. He gives her the basic needs for survival, but she finds herself having to stretch every dollar she earns; she even finds herself having to borrow money, and when things get bad enough, she starts leaning on her boyfriend for money. He gives her the money she needs, but it comes at a price. He's an abusive cheater. If she's going to keep getting money from him, she's going to have to look the other way whenever his phone rings in the middle of the night; she can't ask a lot of questions and she has to do what she's told. She has to tolerate his many tantrums, lies and insecurities. But even in that, he doesn't help her some months because she's made him angry. So, she reaches out to you and asks to borrow some money. You agree to do so, and before long, you become a regular resource for her. But Abba, her Source, wants to drive her out of fornication; the problem is, you're supplying her there. Can you see how your brook (finances) could easily be dried up because of this? The point is, you should never finance or supply someone who is in rebellion. And I know the question that most people will ask behind this. Well, what about those men and women on the street? Should we not show the love of God and help them? There's nothing wrong with helping a person; this is different from becoming a person's personal and continual resource. Your assignment is to give them the Word of God and try to win that soul for Christ. But just as any relationship, you can't allow yourself to become a personal public assistance center, otherwise, the person will tolerate the Word to get his or her needs met. You can partner people up with agencies that will help them, but you don't want to become a supply center for people who want the hand of God, but not the heart of God. This is the quickest way for you to end up in financial ruins.

Just like everything valuable in your life, you have to create boundaries around your finances. And again, it is useless to establish boundaries that you won't consistently enforce. For example, I create seals and logos for ministries. My store has over one thousand available designs. When someone buys a logo or a seal from my store, since it's already designed, I don't need that person's approval. I just add the text that the individual requested and email the design files over to him or her. However, sometimes, people request to change an image or to change the color of a posted design, and of course, they have to pay extra to have this done. Whenever this happens, I don't email the design to them without their approval. I have a system for custom designs, wherein if a customer orders a custom design, I'll create the design, put a watermark on it and upload it to a password protected page on my site. I created a system wherein these particular pages show a thumbnail of the watermarked design. The customer is able to enlarge the thumbnail to look at the details. All the same, there is a set of instructions

Financial Boundaries

just above the design. There are buttons on the site that read:
- Request Revision
- Pay Order Balance
- Approve Sample

The customer can request a revision (if his or her package allows for one), pay the order's balance or approve the design (if the customer paid in full for the design when ordering it). But when a customer orders a design from my store tab, I normally don't upload it to one of these pages because it's already created; they are buying it as-is. If the customer requests changes to the design, I'll make those changes, put a watermark on the design and email it to the customer, along with a note. It would be more professional for me to treat the store-featured designs the same way I treat custom designs, but sometimes, it's just taxing and time-consuming, so I opt to email them the watermarked design with a note requiring that they say "Approve" if they are satisfied with the design. You'd be surprised at the number of people who rebel against this system. Instead, they'll email me back with, "This is great! Thank you!" or "I love it! Thanks! When will I get it?" Here's the note I normally send:

> *Great day to you and thank you for your order. Your new seal (sample) is attached. Please review the design, and if all is well with it, simply reply back with Approved. If you require a revision, simply respond with the details for your revision request. Once you have approved the design, we'll remove the watermark and send you all of the files. Thanks*

> *again for trusting Anointed Fire with your vision.*

Now, like you, I'm very forgiving when a person doesn't follow the rules because it's possible that the customer got too excited or didn't fully read the email. So, I'll email the customer back, saying, "Hi, I'm glad you love the design! Please reply back with Approved and we can release the design to you." I've literally had people emailing me or calling me and yelling, "I said I liked it!" I then explain to the customer that we have to have a record of them approving the design. Nevertheless, this is often countered with, "What's the difference?!" Let me explain to you why I have to be so legalistic in my terms. Customers are allowed up to one free revision with store designs. If a customer does not replay back with "Approved," that customer can easily get two renditions of one logo or seal for the price of one. And yes, people will do this religiously if they can! And will shout about the fact that they got over on you! There have been times (in the infancy of my business) when I'd relaxed those standards to avoid an argument, and it <u>always</u> backfired. *Always.* The customer would get the finalized files and then, request that another change be made to the design. When I'd tell the customer that once we send the finalized files out, they can't request a revision; the customer would have to pay $49, that would not end well. The customer would then shout, "I never said I approved the design! I just said I liked it!" This play on words taught me to honor and enforce my own boundaries religiously and without fail. Every time I've failed to honor one of my own rules, but instead relaxed my standards because the customer was nice or I didn't feel like dealing with the headache of an emotionally unstable customer, that transaction ended up costing me dearly. I would end up spending, at minimum, four times the amount of time on that particular order than I normally spend on logo and seal orders. I soon learned that the reason boundaries are important is because they keep lawless people at bay. Only bound people hate boundaries. In truth, boundary-hating people have closed more businesses than any other force on the face of this planet. Of course, it's the owners' fault for allowing these people to tread on their policies, but the point is—anything of value has to be guarded by a boundary, and that boundary has to be enforced every single day.

And finally, please note that the same key that delivers you from poverty is a master key that opens the door of your wealthy place. You have to give God the key to each city, and He must be allowed to reign over every city and state of you. When He reigns, He causes it to rain. Now, this doesn't mean to declare Him as Lord over those cities and then, go off and serve the enemy. It means that He has to be Lord over those cities; in other words, you have to obey Him, even when you don't understand Him. When God takes His rightful place, deliverance takes place and the enemy is driven out of his places of abode. And slowly, but surely, the Word will advance on every state until you are consumed with His presence. This is a process, but the wait is so worth it.

Deuteronomy 7:22-24: And the LORD thy God will put out those nations before thee by little and little: thou mayest not consume them at once, lest the beasts of the field increase upon thee. But the LORD thy God shall deliver them unto thee, and shall destroy them with a mighty destruction, until they be destroyed. And he shall deliver their kings into thine hand, and thou shalt destroy their name from under heaven: there shall no man be able to stand before thee, until thou have destroyed them.

HEART BOUNDARIES

Matthew 12:43: When the unclean spirit is gone out of a man, he walketh through dry places, seeking rest, and findeth none.

Adulteress. Temptress. Seductress. That was Satan's assignment for me. My maternal grandmother had fallen into that trap. My mother had fallen into that trap. Now, it was my turn, but the problem was, I've always hated the idea of hurting women. I didn't mind hurting (some) men because I'd been hurt by (some) men, but I could relate to women, so I didn't want to be a willing participant in the destruction of any woman's relationship. Nevertheless, I had friends (at that time) who didn't mind having affairs with married or unavailable men. We would often talk about their "indiscretions" and they would share their points of view with me, with the most popular of those perspectives being:
1. "If she was taking care of her man, he wouldn't be interested in me."
2. "He came after me; I didn't go after him!"
3. "I remember when a woman named _____ did that to me! Girl, they'll take your man if they can, so why should I care about their relationship?"

They would go on to speak unspeakable evils over the wife or girlfriend as if those women had wronged them. I was the youngest in the clique, but for whatever reason, they would often refer to me as "Mamma" because I would fuss in some instances and agree in others, but in most cases, I would share my perspective. To them, the woman was the problem; to me, the man was the problem. Nevertheless, it wouldn't be long before curiosity would get the best of me, and I'd find myself wanting to see what it was like to be somebody's mistress.

Let's fast forward to the year 2013. I was saved, sanctified, filled with the Holy Spirit and newly single. I'd finally repented and died to myself; I was no longer the broken shell of a woman I'd once been. She was long gone! I'd just won one of the most intense battles I'd ever endured; that is, I'd finally overcome idolatry several years prior. And hear this—my deliverance hadn't taken place at a church's altar; it took place at the altar of decision. This was done through prayer and taking accountability for my own wrongs and dysfunctions. I was no longer pointing the finger of blame at the people who'd hurt and disappointed me. I had completely forgiven them and erased them from the equation that is my life. All the same, I was more "on fire" for God than I'd ever been in my life.

In 2015, I moved to Georgia from Florida and I was excited about the move because it had been prophesied to me over and over again since 2009. I was finally in the place God had called me to, and I was SURE that everything I'd been praying for was about to materialize within the next 12

Heart Boundaries

months or less. Months into the move, I was beginning to question my decision. I found myself enduring one of the most intense financial attacks of my saved life. My car kept breaking down, and every time I'd take it to a mechanic, they'd fix one thing, only for something else to break less than a week later. These were no minor issues. I was shelling out over a thousand dollars at a time. My Mom had been diagnosed with cancer again, and she'd come to Georgia so that she could go to the Cancer Treatment Centers of America. I'd just gotten an eight thousand dollar bill from the IRS. Everything seemed to be falling apart in my life and I felt powerless to help myself and my mother. God had supernaturally delivered me from debt a few years prior. A foreclosed home, a bunch of repossessed vehicles, unpaid credit card debt and loans had once haunted me; they had been from the decisions I'd made when I was young, immature and reckless. But one day, I'd checked my credit report and it was all gone! All of it! And no, I hadn't paid a credit repair agency. Most of it just fell off. My credit score had gone up by two hundred points, and I was now entering the 700 club. I was excited because I was truly experiencing some very pronounced miracles in my life. I'd repented of fornication some years earlier when I had been married, and I'd renounced it. I was finally starting to see the fruit of my new heart! But I'd made a major mistake—one that I blamed for the financial chaos I was in. I'd gotten a credit card.

Now, it may sound super deep and religious, but before I'd gotten that card, money seemed to be coming from the

North, the South, the East and the West. I truly owed no man anything but to love him. But one day, I went to Kohl's Department Store to purchase a coat. I had the money for the coat; I was going to pay with my debit card, but when I got to the register, the clerk asked me if I wanted a Kohl's card. At first, I said no. She then told me the benefits of getting the card and how it would help my credit. Normally, I would reiterate my "no" when a clerk tried to get me to sign up for a credit card. I'd tell them how I was debt-free for the first time in my life, and I would excitedly tell them about the benefits of living debt-free. But on this day, something was different. I wanted to buy a house, and I needed to reestablish my credit to do so. My credit score was good, but I hadn't charged anything for nearly a decade, so my high credit score was pretty much useless. In that moment, I became like Eve. I looked at the flyer on the counter about the Kohl's card. I considered it, and all of a sudden, I blurted out, "Okay! Let's do it." The next day, I started having car trouble, and a week later, I was darn near broke. This attack went on for a while, and I prayed and prayed to find out the direction of the attack. That's when I remembered the credit card. Had I opened up my finances to the evil one, after all, God does say to owe no man nothing but to love him. Had I allowed myself to be seduced back into the bondage God had delivered me from? Or was I being too deep? Either way, I decided to pay off that card and cut it into tiny, unrecognizable pieces, but by this time, the damage had been done. And while in the middle of this financial attack, a doorbell rang, but it wasn't the doorbell on the outside of my apartment. It was the doorbell of my heart.

I'd been prophesied to a few months earlier that God was about to send a man into my life, and by the end of that year, I would be married to that man. I'd received this prophecy on a conference call I'd been invited to teach on; there were more than three hundred people on that call. I'd received those words with gladness, and they woke something up in me that should have remained asleep at that time. I'd undergone a divorce nearly two years prior, and for the first time in my life, I was content and focused, but once I heard that prophetic word, my heart shifted and all of a sudden, I found myself having an appetite for marriage. A month or two later, I would receive another prophecy about my husband being a doctor who was on the heels of finding me. But then, the financial attack happened and I could no longer focus on marriage. In all honesty, that attack almost made me renounce the husband God was sending because the dude seemed to be taking far too long, and I was having to weather a lot of HUGE storms by myself. I felt like he was out there, distracted by Jezebel somewhere or fooling around in sin. Little did I know that God was maturing me. He was removing the residue of idolatry from my heart. And then, it happened. I received an inbox message on Facebook from an ex of mine (if I could even call him that). And guess what? The guy was wearing the white jackets that doctors wear and he had a stethoscope wrapped around his neck in the photo! I remember he'd worked in the medical field, but I didn't know how far he'd gone. Could this be him?

Could this be the doctor I'd been prophesied to about? His note read, "I am recently divorced and would like to talk to you. I owe you an apology."

"Duke" wasn't really an ex. Remember, I talked about Satan's plans for me versus God's plans for me. Satan had decided that I'd be nothing more than a seductress, an adulteress and a temptress. Well, with Duke, I'd been a side-chick when I was 18-years old. He had been helping out my brother because he stayed in trouble, and he would often come to my mother's house to visit my brother, but the minute we'd locked eyes, Duke had been smitten, and I say that in the humblest of ways. He was eight-years older than me, but that was a small milestone for Duke. All would have been well except—he had a live-in girlfriend, plus, I didn't like "older men." I was completely and utterly against the whole "side-chick" thing, but I loved messing with Duke's mind, after all, I was a seductress. I drew my self-worth from the attention I received men, and Duke was giving me a lot of it. So, anytime he came over to my mother's house, I would ensnare him all the more. I used to put on the skimpiest of clothes and walk past him. When I told my friends about the older guy who was checking me out, they would laugh and ask me a lot of questions because they knew how silly I was. They knew that I loved to rope men in with seduction, so they would joke that I was about to "mess that man up." And that, I did. I would tease Duke whenever my brother wasn't home. I would light a few candles, play some slow music, and after that, I'd make him go home. I'm only sharing this so you'll understand the story I'm about to share with you. I had absolutely no plans to become romantically involved with Duke, but after months of playing games, I let my guards down and Duke and I began having an affair. And the minute that affair started, I could finally somewhat relate to my friends, only, I didn't hate Duke's girlfriend, nor did I want to steal him away from her. I was just a young woman exploring the depths of my feminine powers, and now that I'm older and wiser, I can truly say that I was exploring the lengths of whatever demonic powers I had. But after a couple of months or so, I'd ended my relationship with Duke because he was getting too serious, plus, I'd had a pregnancy scare. Duke wanted to have a child; I didn't. Duke was getting serious; I wasn't. I felt like he was either trying to get rid of his girl and trade her in for a younger woman, or he thought I'd be some silent woman on the sidelines, having his babies and waiting for his call. Either way, I was offended at the idea, so I ended the relationship. Now, there I was twenty years later reading an inbox message from Duke himself. "What kinda testimony would that be?" I remember thinking to myself. I even joked to my friends about how I'd be giving hope to side-chicks all around the world if I went forward with that relationship. Anyhow, I responded to Duke, and before we exchanged numbers, I said to him, "I am divorced. The old me is completely dead, so I hope you didn't like her too much. Call me and we'll catch up."

Duke called, and it didn't take me long to realize that he was still "under the spell" the old me had put him under. When people are "in love," they aren't truly in love, they are under the influence of another person; this is what the Bible calls intoxicated. In other words, they are not of a sober mind. Duke wasted no time telling me how crazy he used to be about me and how hurt he'd been when our relationship abruptly ended. He didn't realize how different of a person I was; he didn't realize that I was hearing his words from a different perspective. This was a perspective I hadn't had when I was young, dumb, arrogant and bound. All the same, he said something that reassured me that he wasn't the "one" as we like to say. He said, "My divorce should be final any day now." I interrupted him quickly; I think I probably sounded like I had PTSD. I let him know where I stand as a believer. I told him that the old Tiffany is dead and buried and that I didn't entertain married men or recent divorcees. Anyhow, I spoke with him for a total of three days, and each day, I would keep reiterating that I was not the one for him. In all truth, I loved being pursued, especially by someone I'd once known. And of course, the Lord kept rebuking me, telling me to distance myself from Duke, but I kept reasoning within myself that my talking to him was harmless fun. I knew he wasn't right or, at minimum, ready for me because he was not in Christ. He said he believed in "the man upstairs," but he wasn't religious. On the third day, I remember hearing a near-audible voice saying, "You are now entering a soul tie." It sounded like the voice of a pilot. I panicked. I'd come too far to fall back into the pits God had delivered me from! All the same, I didn't want to ruin my chances of meeting the man God was sending my way simply because I liked how it felt to be heavily pursued again. So, I told Duke that he could no longer call me. We argued about my decision, and his last words to me were something to the effect of, "One day, when we're in our seventies, you're going to look back on this day and regret this. We're going to get married at a nursing home, and people are going to ask us what took us so long, and I'm gonna say, 'She didn't believe I was the one. She let religion separate her from true love.'" His words would have made the old me think twice, but the creature I'd become knew how poetic Satan could be. This isn't to say that he was the devil; it is to say that the enemy was playing matchmaker, and I wasn't about to fall for it again.

Adulteress. Temptress. Seductress. Again, this was Satan's assignment for me. One thing I learned about Satan is this—once he decides what he wants you to be, he doesn't back down from it. If he decides that you will be a bona fide whore, that's what he will pursue in you. He'll break your self-worth down until you finally come into agreement with him. In my case, that old familiar spirit had strategically set me up to return to the vomit that God had delivered me from.

- First, I'd gone under a huge financial attack. While talking with Duke, I kept thinking about how all of my money troubles would be a thing of the past if I were to date him.
- Next, there were those "prophecies." Now, don't get me wrong—now that I know more about the prophetic, I realize that it could have been God speaking, but then again, a possibility has two sides

to it. Those prophecies woke something up in me; they pretty much prepared the way for Duke's arrival, after all, one of them said my husband was a doctor. Duke was one step away from being a doctor.

Satan had been advancing through my financial state, and he'd started crossing over into my Eros state, but to step over that boundary, he needed me to enter into another agreement. I can almost see him, standing at the border, holding up the forbidden fruit. "One more step," he hisses as I walked towards the edge of sound reasoning. "You're almost there!" But then, God stepped in and began to strengthen me. I looked at the once beautiful fruit on the other side, and all of a sudden, it started looking like dung to me. I walked away with a defeated and devastated devil howling as I rejected him once again. He realized in that moment that it was truly over and I was never coming back to him. Ever!

Satan had a blueprint of what I was to become, and at one point in my life, he watched as his plans for me unfolded. But God had strategically placed people in my midst who'd demonstrated another way of life—one that was foreign to me—one that involved the One I wanted the most, and that is God. I'd been married twice because of adultery. What's amazing is, Satan knew that he couldn't get me into downright adultery, so he had to use a technique similar to what many of us pet owners use. When we're trying to give a pill to a dog, we often have to wrap meat around that pill so that the dog doesn't see it. Because the dog has a keen sense of smell, we have to rely on the dog's anxiousness to get that meat out of our hands, and this often works. I've hidden pills in hot dogs and given them to my dog, and without paying attention, he's gulped the hot dog down. Eventually, he got privy to this so I had to use a different technique. Satan had to disguise adultery in order for me to fall into it because I despised it so much. So, when I met my first husband-to-be, he was married but going through a divorce. I justified our relationship by telling myself that I hadn't ruined his marriage and the two of them were already broken up before I entered the picture. They were just waiting on a judge to sign the final divorce decree. Nevertheless, this was outright adultery and I paid a huge price for it! But did I learn my lesson? Nope! While going through a divorce from him, I continued in the generational curse of not knowing how to be alone. I met the next guy I'd call hubby while going through the first divorce. And even though I was more mature as a Christian, I still justified my relationship with him. I paid a hefty price for that decision as well. And now, there that devil was again, ringing the doorbell of my heart, and I opened the door and let it into my conscious. God had warned me that I was entering a soul tie, so I ended those communications before I found myself back in romantic bondage.

While talking to Duke, Satan was advancing against my heart, but right before I'd ended my communications with him, I'd asked him a question in my attempt to prove to him that he was looking for a dead woman. I asked him, "What do you miss about me? When you think of me, what do you think of?" I smiled as I waited for his answer, and not because I was flattered. I smiled because I knew he wouldn't be able to answer that question without incriminating himself and proving me right. He'd thought about it for a minute, and then, sighed. "Oh my. You're right! I can't believe this! I do think about you lying in my arms! Oh wow!" He missed the seductive, feisty and confident woman I'd once been. Don't get me wrong; my self-esteem was shot, but my confidence was through the roof. How is that possible? I didn't know who I was! My confidence was in my reflection; my confidence was in my femininity! After proving my point, I could feel the power of God and the love of God overtaking me. "I release you from that spell in the name of Jesus!" I said aloud. I realized that the spell I'd placed on him through seduction was just as powerful that day as it had been twenty years prior. I started using the power of declaration to break those chains off his life, and even though I probably sounded like a crazy woman to him, I realized in that moment what God wanted me to do. I had to release someone who I'd once seduced because he had never gotten free, even though I had. The enemy had sent him to bind me, but God used that opportunity to set him free. At least, spiritually, that is. He still reached out to me a few times, claiming that I was "the one."

Guard your heart, for out of it pours the issues of life. When Satan decides that you will be, for example, a mass

Heart Boundaries

murderer, he will stop at nothing to conform and deform you until you fit into the mold he's created for you. He'll use whatever tools he can to hurt, manipulate and break you. This is why God told us to guard our hearts. In other words, create and enforce boundaries around your ears and your eyes! Again, this is the subconscious mind, but in order for the enemy to get to the heart, he has to go through the conscious mind, which is the waiting room of your soul. To date, I warn both women and men about the power of communication. Soul ties aren't always created through sex; you can end up in soul tie just by communicating with someone frequently. You also need to know that there are one-sided soul ties, just as there are two-sided soul ties. A one-sided soul tie is a relationship where a person is bound to a person mentally, emotionally, financially or spiritually who is not bound to him or her. A perfect example of this is a common trap that the millennial generation often falls into. This trap is an old one, but today, it is disguised as "friendship." The way that it works is:

1. A man approaches a woman that he is romantically or sexually attracted to.
2. He expresses interest in that woman, and the two of them exchange phone numbers.
3. He asks the woman out on a date. After the date or after he's gotten the woman's hopes up, he says to her, "I'm not ready for a relationship right now, but I would like us to be friends and I want to hang out with you from time to time. I really enjoyed your company."
4. The woman is confused, but reluctantly agrees,

hoping that he'll come to see her value and change his mind about her. This doesn't happen. Ever.
5. This arrangement continues until the man either finds a woman he is truly interested in, he finds a woman who won't agree to this arrangement or the woman who agreed to passively date him decides to free herself from his web of deceit.

And men aren't the only creatures who do this. Women pull this stunt too. And it's hard to tell someone not to accept an undefined arrangement, because nowadays, millennials will shout back, "Well, we have to be friends first!" And while I agree, you must understand the very definition of a friend. In this case, the man in question isn't looking to be a friend. He's collecting women. Someone who wants to be your friend will just be friendly, and if he exchanges numbers with you, he is intentional about not leading you on. If he is romantically interested in you, but wants to get to know you before pursuing a relationship, he won't sit in the waiting room of your romantic state. He'll come through your platonic state and get to know you from there. In other words, he won't confuse you! Confusion is a red flag; it often indicates that you are dealing with someone who is either mildly narcissistic or extremely narcissistic. For example, if a man is romantically interested in me, but wants to take things slowly (which is the best practice, of course), chances are, he'll find something that makes us relatable. He'll ask for my number and start establishing a friendship with me. Once he realizes that he truly wants to pursue a relationship, he'll talk to me about it. This is the normal route, but of course, not all men go in this direction. To get you off the market, some men come through the romantic state, but while they're there, they'll loudly proclaim, "Remember, we're just friends! Nothing more!" They'll sit in the conscious or the waiting room of the romantic state; that is, until the woman opens her heart (subconscious) and allows them in. Once they've created value in her life, they'll start advancing on her romantically, all the while, reminding her that they want nothing more than a friendship. Listen, there is nothing new under the sun! The oldest men on Earth can tell you that this game is older than they are! But why advance on a woman's heart romantically? I often use this example. Imagine a man walking through a retail store shopping for pleasure, affirmation, wholeness and a host of other void-fillers. He comes across you. You're a beautiful and interesting doll that commands his attention. He wants you, but he's not sure how or if you would be a good fit for his life because he doesn't fully know or understand the fullness of what he wants just yet. Your price tag is high. He has to decide in that moment if he's willing to pay the full price for you; that is, if you don't lower your value. He decides that you cost more than he's willing to pay, after all, he believes that he can find someone better than you at a lower price. He just hasn't come across her yet. The only problem is—you're a catch; you're a steal, and you're the only version of you on the market! He knows that someone is going to come along, see your worth and snatch you off the shelf. He worries that he'll see this man enjoying the benefits of being with you and he'll never find this perfect girl he's been looking for. He worries that he'll regret the day he passed you by, so he grabs you off the shelf and puts you in his shopping cart. He begins carting you around for a few months or a few years (however long you'll let him), but one day, he realizes that the time to make a decision regarding you is drawing nigh because the store is about to close. Other men come in the store looking for a woman like you, but you're in his cart, being taking for a ride. The time finally comes for him to checkout, so he takes you to the register and puts everything else on the conveyor belt that's of importance to him. He puts his friends on the conveyor belt, he puts his money on the conveyor belt and he puts his family on the conveyor belt. "How much is that?" he asks. The cashier gives him the price. "Okay," he says without hesitation. "Here, I don't want her. Put her back." Now, you're in a return cart, crying and regretting your decision to be carted around for a few months or a few years. And because he's dropped you a few times, you have a few bumps and bruises from the ride, so they can't just put you back on the shelf. They have to return you to the Manufacturer for repair; that is, if you're not so impatient that you insist on just being sold "as is" at a discounted rate.

I've seen countless millennials falling into this trap, and I've tried to warn them, but all too often, they'll brush it off, saying something like, "No, I'm cool with us just being friends." So, I shrug my shoulders and change the conversation. This is their lesson to learn, not mine. Months later, they reach out to me brokenhearted and trying to figure out how to get out of a soul tie, not realizing that a soul tie, when it is ungodly, is nothing but a rope used to ensnare them. Narcissists love to create soul ties with people; they use time, intimacy, gifts and promises to create and strengthen these soul ties. The question then becomes—well, how do you initiate a romantic relationship in the 21st century? In the right state. A man can't meet me and immediately start approaching the Eros or romantic state; that's reserved for my husband. He has to approach me platonically and spiritually; this way, there is no confusion. A relationship that is not defined has no borders or limitations, which means, it has no rules. Anything that has no definition is reckless and dangerous! So, let's say a guy is romantically interested in you. He wants to get to know you for the sake of building a relationship with you, but of course, the both of you are mature and you want to start off with a friendship and evolve into a relationship from there. How is this done?

1. Both of you have to be clear with one another regarding your expectations.
2. You have to define a time or a grace that's acceptable for you, and he has to do the same. In other words, you can say, for example, "We can build a friendship for about six months. After that, we need to revisit the matter." If after six months, he's still saying that he wants to be friends, let him go! Men are the surest creatures on the face of this planet! You can ask any sound man and he will confirm this. If after six months, he's still unsure, the truth is that he's sure he doesn't want you, but you are that proverbial doll in

the cart at this point. He's carting you around until he finds someone better.
3. Be accountable with your friendship; keep your mentors and/or leaders informed and up-to-date with your relationship. Ask questions and be open to hear and properly respond to the truth. In other words, if your pastor says, "He's playing games! It's up to you, of course, but if I were you, I'd release him," the best thing to do is to follow your pastor's advice. Understand that narcissistic, jezebellic folks will NEVER release you. They will keep manipulating you until you either realize your worth or they find someone else they feel is better than you. And even then, they won't fully let you go. They'll keep popping in and out of your life from time-to-time to make sure that their seats are still unoccupied.
4. Test the spirit of the person; this is biblical! And do not ignore the fruit that you see! Study the fruits of the Holy Spirit and check to see if those fruits are present and ripe in that person's life.

Again, you are divided up into many states. They are your:
1. Mental state
2. Physical state
3. Religious state
4. Parental state
5. Familial state
6. Relational state
7. Romantic state

8. Sexual state
9. Career state
10. Financial state

All of these states surround your soul; this is the housing center of your heart of hearts. Every state has its own heart, and the enemy seeks to advance into the pulpit or the cockpit of every one of these states. But overall, his desire is to enter your heart; this is your mind. This is the part of you that controls, fuels and empowers every part of you. And he doesn't have to get to this state romantically. He can come through your family, your friends, your finances or whatever area of your life that is unguarded. He loves the romantic state because your romantic state is like the state of Texas; it is huge and it largely influences your emotional economy. When the heart is unguarded, every state of a man will be compromised. This is why Proverbs 25:28 says, "He that hath no rule over his own spirit is like a city that is broken down, and without walls."

Heart boundaries are necessary for survival; they are also necessary if you want to remain sane. And one way to draw heart boundaries is by creating what I call labels. Again, every relationship needs definition. Every relationship has to have boundaries, restrictions, allowances, benefits and disadvantages. For example, the benefit of being in a relationship with you can be:
- The guy gets to talk to you daily.
- The guy gets to spend time with you.

- The guy gets to hold your hand.
- The guys gets to court you exclusively.

Of course, the only disadvantage is that he cannot get husband privileges. A guy who wants to be a friend, on the other hand, doesn't get these benefits.

- You speak with him when you have the time.
- You hang out (publicly) with him when you're available to do so, but whenever you start courting someone, this may have to end. (In truth, I wouldn't hang out with him. I use this logic—I refuse to allow another man to park in my husband's parking space. I need that space to be unoccupied when he arrives).
- He cannot touch your hand or any part of your body.
- He cannot keep you from meeting and getting to know other guys.

Now, if he gets the benefits of courtship while calling himself a friend, he will essentially become a friend with benefits; this means that he has the title of a friend, but he's enjoying the benefits of a role that he refuses to enter. And today, there are millions of men and women out there in undefined relationships; they call these "arrangements" friends with benefits, but in truth, they are nothing but two people pleasing one another physically while they wound each other mentally and emotionally. In these types of relationships, oftentimes the woman's self-esteem, self-worth and self-perception are all damaged, and what she doesn't realize is that Satan is using those encounters to mold her into the woman he's decided that she should be. The same is true for the guy. It needs to be understood that Satan has a blueprint of who he says you will be, and the sad part is, most Christians have allowed him, through pain, rejection, abandonment and impatience, to wound them until they finally became what he wanted them to be. This is when you see people posting stuff up like, "I tried to be nice, but folks don't understand kindness, so from here on out, I'm gonna be _____." They'll often say they're going to be coldhearted, promiscuous or disloyal. This means that they've now crossed the boundary; they are now in a greater level of bondage. What I've witnessed is that most people refuse to draw or enforce boundaries around their hearts and their lives because doing so would mean they'd lose a lot of relationships, including connections with most of their family members. So, they reason within themselves that they have to make accommodations for abuse and tolerate toxicity in order to remain connected with the people they love. Consequently, they spend the rest of their lives being wounded until they are finally in shape to do Satan's will. Please read this carefully—boundaries are designed to DRIVE OUT demons and the folks who love being bound! In other words, boundaries are supposed to drive these folks away! This is why James 4:7 states, "Submit yourselves therefore to God. Resist the devil, and he will flee from you." We've been taught wrong. We were taught to tolerate toxic people who love being manipulative and toxic. Listen, you can love folks from a distance! All the same, putting the proper labels on each relationship, and defining those labels will help you to live a drama-free life filled with peace and

prosperity. You should have the following labels:
1. Friends
2. Close Friend(s)
3. Best Friend(s)
4. Mentors (These are your confidants)
5. Coaches
6. Mentees
7. Brothers and Sisters in Christ
8. Acquaintances
9. Family Members
10. Close Family Members
11. Distant Family Members
12. Estranged Family Members

And here are a few more facts:
1. Mentees are often confused with friends. Any relationship where you find yourself pouring out and helping a person more than that person helps you, please understand that the individual is not your friend. He or she is a mentee. If you call the person a friend, offense is inevitable because, at some point, you're going to start feeling used. Mentees love to use the label of a friend so that they can have a friend's pass to your heart. For example, I won't talk on the phone with a mentee everyday, but I would talk with a friend daily if needed.
2. The difference between a close friend and a best friend is that your best friend is often like a sibling to you, whereas a close friend typically is someone who

you can trust; this is normally a person who you may not speak with often, but you trust him or her with your deepest, most private thoughts, fears and secrets.
3. Every label has to be defined by you. What is a friend to you? What should a friend do and what shouldn't a friend do? How does a friend graduate from a friend to a best friend?
4. You should have allowances and restrictions for every label, for example, for a distant family member, I'm not going to tell that person too much about my life. All the same, that relative cannot move into my home or borrow money from me.
5. Offense is oftentimes the product of someone crossing the boundary between one label to another. People often want the responsibilities of one label, but the benefits of a more intimate label. And if allowed, they will cross these boundaries, for example, when I was new to ministry, I had friends who were really mentees in disguise, but they not only insisted on calling themselves friends, they insisted on calling me their best friend. For a season of my life, I allowed this because I didn't know any better, but I would always end up offended because I realized I was giving far more than I was getting in return. These people would enjoy the perks of friendship, but anytime I needed them, they would run and hide behind the mentee label. They wouldn't call themselves mentees, they'd just start acting nonchalant. I had to put an end to

this. I started calling people what they were based on their fruit. After that, I started enforcing the boundaries associated with those labels, and this wasn't easy because people who are used to having undefined terms hate it when you start limiting their access to you. Nevertheless, I gave them options—be an unmasked acquaintance or a former friend—OR if they insisted on calling me a friend, they would have to start acting as such, meaning, they'd have to give as much as they received or as much as they required.

6. People can get promoted and demoted, but you should never promote someone quickly. You have to be patient and examine that person's fruit over a period of time before you promote that individual. Failing to do so can and will likely end in you getting offended or hurt. A friend can become a close friend, just as a close family member can suddenly become distant. And you have to be okay with allowing people to transition from one label or level to another. All the same, it will take time and a few rebukes for them to get used to their newfound roles, especially if they were demoted in your life. And please note that when I say "demoted," I'm not saying this in a condescending or wrathful way, I'm simply talking about the distance between your heart and theirs; that's all.

7. The difference between a mentor and a coach is this—coaches help you in a specific field (life

coaching, business coaching, book coaching, etc.), but when you get a mentor, you are essentially saying you want an impartation from the mentor. This sounds weird, but it's what Jesus described when He said, "He that eateth my flesh, and drinketh my blood, dwelleth in me, and I in him." In this, He is dealing with the world of impartation, after all, this is what mentorship is about. The mentor doesn't just deal with a specific area of the mentee's life, the mentor deals with every area of the mentee's life. When you sign up for mentorship, what you're essentially saying to the mentor is, "I see the calling, the anointing and the grace that's on your life, and I want to partner with it!" By doing so, you partake of and even inherit this same grace. This is what Elisha did when he followed and submitted to Elijah. When Elijah was about to be taken up, Elisha asked for a double portion of his anointing.
8. Whenever someone keeps crossing between two states illegally, this should serve as a red flag to you. I can't say this enough—bound people hate boundaries!

The goal of these labels is to help you clearly define roles and responsibilities in your life. This lessens the amount of offense that you have to endure as the result of having undefined relationships. It also helps you to properly guard your heart.

Another way to guard your heart is through the casting down of imaginations. What are imaginations? They are a nation of images (some still, some animated) that play in our minds; they often produce:

Good	Bad
Perfect Love/Courage/Boldness	Fear/Paranoia/Suspicion
Patience	Anxiousness/Impatience/Anxiety
Hope	False Hope
Faith	Sin
Kindness	Offense
Obedience	Disobedience

Most heart-hijacks come through the imagination. When the enemy is on the border or the boundary between one state and another, one of his most effective and quickest ways to cross those lines is to create a mental advertisement for the person to see and meditate on. A great example of this happens in our churches, and they often happen to Christian women who don't know how to properly steer their imaginations. For example, a woman has been attending her church for years, but lately, something in her has changed. She appears to be "glowing" as some would say. As it turns out, there's a guy at her church who's been giving her a little or a lot of attention. He appears to be single and sold out for

Heart Boundaries

the Lord. Now, there's nothing wrong with having a crush on someone, but crushes have the power to crush your self-esteem if you don't know how to manage your mind. Anyhow, every time the guy sees this particular woman, he speaks to her, cracks a few jokes and stares as she walks away. One day, he even speaks of the future with her; he says, "You're going to make a great mother!" She walks away, smiling, flattered and hopeful. To her, it would seem that he's prophetically speaking of their future children or, at minimum, he's making plans for "their" future together. Is this flirting? Yeah, maybe. But does this mean that he wants to pursue a relationship with her and thinks that she may be "the one?" It's possible, but unlikely. She leaves church excited and ready to call her best friend. "Girl, you won't believe what Wyatt said to me!" she shouts excitedly. From there, she fills her friend in on Wyatt's new antics, after all, she's been keeping her friend in the loop.

One beautiful Sunday morning, Chloe shows up at church, eagerly anticipating Wyatt's arrival. She's cut and colored her hair, plus, she's wearing a new dress and a pair of six-inch stilettos. All the same, she had her friend to paint her face with makeup because she was sure that this day would be the day Wyatt finally asked for her number. She steps into the church, smelling like a bed of sun-kissed roses, but Wyatt hasn't arrived yet. She lounges around in the hallway, hoping to see him or, better yet, for him to see her. During her second bathroom break, she captures a glimpse of Wyatt's back. He's standing at the entryway of the church, talking and laughing. Chloe walks up to her crush and clears her throat. Wyatt turns around and is taken aback by Chloe's new look, but he can't say much, after all, he has brought a visitor to church with him. "Oh wow! Chloe, you look great," he says as he holds the door open for a beautiful young woman who can't seem to stop laughing. "Whatever!" laughs the beautiful young stranger, looking Wyatt in the eyes. "That's okay. Next time, I'll wear a hijab and pretend to be Muslim! I'll just say to your mother, 'As salamu alaykum, Ms. Payne. And I'll make sure to avoid eye contact with your father! Let's see how funny you will be then!" The beautiful stranger walks through the door and it becomes even more clear that she's there with Wyatt. Wyatt laughs as he closes the door. "Excuse my girlfriend, Sister Chloe. I think she got dropped one too many times when she was a baby," he jokes before introducing the two women. "Oh yeah, September, this is Chloe. Chloe, this is September, my fiance."

> "Did he just call me Sister Chloe? And did he just call her his fiance?!"

Chloe struggles to regain her composure and purge the frown lines from her face. "It's nice to meet you," she stutters.

For the rest of the service, Chloe is distracted, hurt, embarrassed and offended. How dare he lead her on! Her phone vibrates a few minutes before service ends. It's a text from her best friend. "How did it go? I can't wait to hear the latest episode!" Chloe responds with a sad-face emoji. "I'll

Heart Boundaries

call you when I leave," she responds.

For the next few weeks, Chloe finds herself speaking against Wyatt's relationship. "I don't know what he sees in that Jezebel!" she says to her sister one day. "I just know what God showed me! I keep dreaming about this man, and I've said to God, 'Lord, if he's not the one, take him out of my heart or give me a sign,' and God hasn't said anything! Normally, when I pray that prayer, God will give me a sign or I'll just wake up and those old feelings would be gone, but for whatever reason, He hasn't said anything! I keep trying to convince myself that Wyatt isn't the one, but every time I do this, I end up dreaming about him. Just the other day, I dreamed that he was holding a beautiful baby girl, and he said to me, 'I think she needs to be breastfed.' She looked just like him!" As the days and the weeks pass her by, she graduates from speaking against Wyatt's relationship to praying against it. In other words, she unknowingly begins to practice witchcraft. And what she doesn't know is that witchcraft is in her blood. Her great-grandmother was a witch; her grandmother toyed around with the dark arts and her mother played with witchcraft. So, the enemy decided that Chloe would be a full-blown witch, but he had to find a way to activate what was already in her. I can't tell you how many women I've witnessed fall into this very trap! He uses their imaginations to lure them into his plans for them. He entered into their romantic states through the waiting room of their imaginations, and from there, he proceeded to enter their religious states. Chloe reasoned within herself that

Wyatt's new girlfriend was a witch assigned by hell to interrupt and intercept God's plans for her and Wyatt. This is actually more common of a scenario than we care to admit. This is why it is imperative that we draw boundaries even around our imaginations. This is why 2 Corinthians 10:5 says, "Casting down imaginations, and every high thing that exalteth itself against the knowledge of God, and bringing into captivity every thought to the obedience of Christ." Imaginations can be fun, but they can also be dangerous. You should never use your imagination to hijack the will of another human being; this is also why God warns us in Matthew 6:34, "Take therefore no thought for the morrow: for the morrow shall take thought for the things of itself. Sufficient unto the day is the evil thereof."

One of the reasons God tells us to guard our hearts is because when there is an attack against the heart, the soul (mind, will and emotions) can respond by splitting. In the medical world, they call these splits:
- Dissociative Identity Disorder (formerly known as Multiple Personality Disorder)
- Schizophrenia (means split mind)
- Bipolar Disorder

These are just a short list of the disorders created when a heart suffers the impact of a demonic attack.

A split in the heart is called a void. Merriam Webster defines a void as:
- opening, gap

- empty space : emptiness, vacuum
- the quality or state of being without something: lack, absence
- a feeling of want or hollowness

A void looks like that big empty space between the streets in the dream that I described earlier. Remember, I talked about one street being split down the middle, and I was on one side of the street. My ex or, better yet, a demonic spirit disguising itself as an ex was on the other side of the street. He couldn't get to me and I couldn't get to him. That big empty space is a bottomless pit; it separates one world from another. Additionally, had I tried to cross that boundary, I would have fallen into that pit. All the same, a void is very similar. There are two types of voids. They are:

1. A lack of information. I imagine these voids looking like air pockets within a soul.
2. A wound or split in the soul.

Lack of Information

Voids represent a lack of light (revelation); that is a lack of information. This is why God said, "My people perish for lack of knowledge." I like to think of it as a soft spot on a newborn baby's skull. That spot has to be protected, so when the parents hold the child, they typically hold the head (authority) of the child, but right near the crane of the neck, since the top or center of the head has not yet hardened. These voids represent immaturity, and this is why we need pastors to cover us, especially in these areas. It is not uncommon for people to highlight and promote the states that they're good in, all the while, avoiding accountability and confrontation in the states that they are immature in. Because of this, when the enemy wants to attack them, he goes after their soft spots; he goes after those areas that are filled with darkness. Once he attacks those areas, he secures his position by provoking and evoking pride in the person. Pride is hardheartedness. This is when the skull begins to harden, but the problem with this is, the skull has been deformed or conformed to this world.

A Wound or Split in the Soul
Soul splits or wounds are usually the result of trauma or unhealed hurts. Most of these splits are mild, and the majority of people who have them lead semi-normal lives, however, all voids have a gravitational pull. We call these pulls attractions. So, if I had a split or a void created by the absence of a father in my life, that split would be found in my parental state. Consequently, I would likely find myself attracted to either older men, controlling men or men I could control. And whenever I entered a relationship with a guy, he'd have to fill multiple roles, with the most prominent of those roles being a father-figure. This perverted relationship would be somewhat incestuous and pedophilic, even though I'm a grown woman. This is because the wound would have stunted my growth both mentally and emotionally. As a result of this, if I married the guy, I wouldn't be physically attracted to him for long. Sex would only serve as a means to keep my husband/father-figure around. He'd be a void-filler. Another

way to say this is, I'd be using him as a human bandage. It goes without saying that he would be unable to fill that void, which is why women who marry their father-figures end up:

1. Arguing a lot. Their husbands don't have peace because they are trying to wear a pair of shoes that they simply cannot fit.
2. Crying a lot. Women who have father-sized voids often fear being rejected, abandoned or betrayed. As a result, the little girl in them manifests herself whenever those fears are highlighted or heightened.
3. Using threats of divorce to regain control. These threats are often the product of the unfulfilled spouses' overactive imagination. The woman may find herself imagining being rescued by a man who understands her and goes out of his way to make her happy. Her threats are just her using one of the many spirits in her arsenal to regain control of what she perceives to be an out-of-control situation. Of course, the spirit that she would be using in this case would be the spirit of fear.
4. Committing adultery. Voids are like huge, bottomless pits; there's no way you can fill them. Only God can do this. So, men and women who have parental voids often have trouble remaining faithful or committed to others because they are always trying to quench the appetites of their voids. Needless to say, there's no way to satisfy or fill a bottomless pit!

All the same, voids are like trigger-activated vacuums. For

example, a man can make a great friend; he can honestly be your best friend for years because in his friend or platonic state, he is emotionally healthy, sane and whole. You can build an amazing friendship with this guy and watch him go from relationship to relationship, only for those relationships to end chaotically. One day, the two of you can find yourselves sharing an intimate moment. Maybe, he's going through a breakup and you happen to go over to his house (which is not wise), and while you're comforting him with kind words, all of a sudden, he says to you, "I wish more women were like you." In that moment, he suddenly realizes that you're everything he wants in a woman and more—or, at least, he believes this. The two of you stare at one another, but a wave of discomfort suddenly hits the both of you, so you turn your heads and laugh it off. Five minutes later, his favorite song comes on the radio and he suddenly leaps to his feet. "I love this song!" he says, slow-dancing by himself. You stand to your feet and try to make your way to the restroom, but he grabs your hand and pulls you close to him. "Come on, dance with me!" he says. "This is my song!" The two of you dance for a minute before you pull away, and once again, the two of you lock eyes. In that moment, he suddenly does the unthinkable. He kisses you. Why did this happen? For one, the void in his romantic state has been activated and enlarged by his breakup. Relationships formed immediately after a breakup are referred to as rebound relationships. It's like a dent in a Coke bottle; it's the broken person's attempt to snap back into place. Next, it happened because you suddenly started looking like a void-filler. Now, if you entertain a relationship with this guy, despite what Hollywood depicts on the big screen, chances are, the relationship won't work. This is because he's healthy in the platonic state, but in the romantic state, his soul is in ruins. And wherever you see a bunch of voids or wounds, you will find an unquenchable appetite for attention, affirmation, sex and/or control. This is why so many women and men today regret ruining good friendships by dating their friends.

Another way the vacuum effect is triggered is called intimacy. Now, don't get me wrong, intimacy doesn't necessarily mean sex. After all, you can have sex with someone and not be intimate with that person. We call sex intimacy because we share our nakedness with another person, but true intimacy involves transparency. For example, Dana and Brenda go to the same gym. After seeing each other at the gym a few times, they start having conversations about their lives, their children, their plans for the future and their churches. They find common ground and begin to build a friendship there. The two women exchange social media handles, and before long, they are chatting online. After this, they exchange numbers, and all is well at first. The problem is that Brenda has a huge wound in her platonic state, but that wound is in the subconscious or the deepest (most intimate part) of that state. As long as Dana was in the waiting room (Brenda's conscious mind), everything was okay. Brenda's void is only triggered whenever people start getting close to her. Dana somehow trips that alarm one day when she says to Brenda, "You're a very dear friend to me. I would even venture out to say that you're quickly becoming one of my best friends." Immediately, Brenda starts feeling warm, excited and most of all, scared. Every friend she's ever had has walked out of her life, so she's socially retarded, for lack of a better term. After this, their friendship reaches an all-time high before it fails miserably. The enemy entered into Dana's life through her physical state, and he used that to advance against her platonically. And now, the women have matching wounds, even though they are no longer friends. Hurt people hurt people, especially in the areas where they've been hurt.

Now that Dana's been wounded platonically, she slowly but surely becomes more and more withdrawn from people. But one day, she goes to the bank and meets a man there. The guy's name is Patrick. The two strike up a conversation while waiting in line about savings accounts, after all, Dana is there to deposit her paycheck into her savings account. They talk about the importance of creating a nest egg for the future and the importance of good credit. After Dana makes her transaction, Patrick then asks her to wait for him so that he can walk her to her car. She agrees, after all, he seems to be a nice guy. In the parking lot, the two talk for a little while longer before exchanging phone numbers.

Almost immediately, Patrick starts moving in on Dana's romantic state because he doesn't know any other way to build a relationship with a woman he's attracted to. He reasons within himself that he has to hurry up and get her off the market before some other guy does. Dana reciprocates his advances and the two immediately begin building a relationship with one another. What's amazing is, they seem to be very compatible, both financially and romantically, so after a year of courting, the two decide to get married. But you have to remember that platonically, Dana is a mess. She was wounded by Brenda and she never got the healing she needed to move on. Please understand that soulish wounds are not like wounds on the body; they don't heal by themselves over time. You need information to stuff into those wounds; this way, you won't keep blaming the person who hurt you for the wound, but you will, instead, take responsibility for your lack of discernment in regards to that person.

Dana and Patrick get married, and all is well at first, but they soon realize the importance of building a friendship. Of course, this should have been the first area that they started building in, but Patrick was in a rush to build a relationship with Dana. The more Patrick shares with Dana, the more paranoid, insecure and fearful she becomes because she knows that she has to reciprocate. She doesn't want to talk about her past or open up about anything she considers to be her business; she clearly doesn't want to be Patrick's friend. She just wants to be his wife, his lover, the mother of his children and his financial partner. Howbeit, the more Patrick advances on her platonically, the more unstable she becomes. What Patrick doesn't know is that he's triggering an alarm within his wife. Because the two are unable to build a friendship, their marriage suffers a fatal blow. One of

Patrick's female co-workers is able to build a friendship with him, and this makes her more and more attractive to Patrick. The two end up having an affair, and Patrick leaves Dana to be with his co-worker. Now, Dana is wounded both platonically and romantically. When Patrick failed to build a friendship with Dana, he neglected to honor Luke 14:28 (ESV), which reads, "For which of you, desiring to build a tower, does not first sit down and count the cost, whether he has enough to complete it?" He didn't count the cost because he didn't know how expensive that relationship would be to his soul! He didn't have enough love in him to complete his broken wife. All the same, it's clear that Patrick was wounded romantically, which is why he chose to cheat. Now, his wound could have been there before he got married, or it's possible that Dana wounded him romantically. Either way, the wound had a strong gravitational pull that Dana could not satisfy. Patrick's new girl will soon discover that she can't satisfy or fix that void either. And if neither party takes accountability and gets the information and help they need to heal, their voids will only grow bigger. This causes them to become more attractive, because people with heart wounds often mask those wounds with makeup, wigs, muscles and smiles. They will attract more people and be attracted to more people; they will wound more people and be wounded by more people.

The heart has to be covered so that it can mature and so that it can heal. This takes time, which means it takes patience. Patience is the grace and the space we give our wounds to heal. If you're impatient, you'll run out there and reenter another friendship, another relationship or another agreement, not realizing that your voids will eventually be triggered, either because you lack the information to sustain whatever it is that you entered, someone triggers that void through intimacy or pain or it'll be triggered by the time-factor.

What is the time-factor? It is both a lease and a leash. It is the amount of time a person can remain in a relationship, be it romantic, platonic or on any plane. For example, in the United States, a governor's term is four years. He can serve two terms if elected, but he can't serve more than eight years. After this, a new governor has to be elected. Remember, you are the governor of every one of your personal states, however, you can relinquish your seat to someone or something else. When this happens, you have relinquished your authority and your authenticity. This means that Hollywood can take this seat, your parents can take this seat, Mammon can take this seat, fear can take this seat, perversion can take this seat and the list goes on. Whoever sits on that seat of your heart in any given state will determine the state of your relationships in that state. For example, there are some men and women who have never been in a romantic relationship past five years. If you look at their family's history, you may see this pattern in their family as well. This means that they were never truly developed in that area; in other words, they weren't taught to love another person as they love themselves, they weren't taught to persevere and they weren't taught how to humble themselves and get the help they need whenever their relationships took a bad turn. Consequently, they are oftentimes very loving, romantic, humble and understanding at the beginning of a relationship, but again, they are both on a lease and a leash. A lease because the enemy has given them a relationship-curfew; a leash because generationally speaking, they don't know how to get past certain issues. So, while they often build relationships that they have every intention of continuing in, they lack the knowledge and the tools needed to stick around beyond a certain point. This is why you have to ask the necessary questions whenever you meet people. All the same, as the governor of each of your personal states, you have to be honest with yourself regarding the conditions of those states.

Guard your heart. An unguarded heart is attractive to the enemy. A mentor once said to me, "Never think the devil will walk past an open door. No! If he sees an opportunity, he's going to take it!" If your heart isn't guarded in every area, Satan will begin to advance against you until he has consumed you. Take this time to assess the damage done in an area of your life, and then, get the help you need so that you can finally become whole. Once you make the necessary investments to heal, including counseling and reading books, you'll learn to value each area of your life. You'll learn to catch people, spirits and thoughts in the waiting room of your conscious and kick them out the minute they prove themselves to be weapons formed against you.

At the same time, you'll learn to pay attention to the areas that people try to enter in and how they try to enter in; this is how discernment is activated! Discernment is not you noticing someone being fidgety or them avoiding eye contact; these are learned skills! Discernment is your ability to test fruit while it is yet in the waiting room! Guard your heart, for out of it flows the issues of life!

YOUR NEIGHBORHOOD OF THINKING

Let's revisit the scene in the Garden of Eden. Genesis 2:16-17 reads, "And the LORD God commanded the man, saying, Of every tree of the garden thou mayest freely eat: But of the tree of the knowledge of good and evil, thou shalt not eat of it: for in the day that thou eatest thereof thou shalt surely die." Theologians and conspiracy theorists have theorized that God gave the instructions to Adam, not Eve! They said that Adam had failed to communicate these instructions with Eve. This is a poorly decorated lie! Let's look at Eve's encounter with Lucifer. Genesis 3:1-3 reads, "Now the serpent was more subtil than any beast of the field which the LORD God had made. And he said unto the woman, Yea, hath God said, Ye shall not eat of every tree of the garden? And the woman said unto the serpent, We may eat of the fruit of the trees of the garden: But of the fruit of the tree which is in the midst of the garden, God hath said, Ye shall not eat of it, neither shall ye touch it, lest ye die." Eve clearly knew what God said, whether Adam told her, God told her or not. She'd crossed a boundary that God had specifically told her not to cross, and like me, she'd ended up dealing with the consequence behind her choice to rebel, only, her sting wouldn't come from a bunch of bees; it would come from death. "The sting of death is sin; and the strength of sin is the law" (1 Corinthians 15:56). When the couple sinned, everyone tried to shift the blame. Adam blamed Eve, and

Eve blamed the devil. But they were both wrong. Adam was wrong for disobeying God, just as Eve was wrong for disobeying God. No one took responsibility for their actions. And because the couple sinned, they were kicked out of the Garden, meaning, they were placed on the other side of a boundary. They were placed under the curse of time! Genesis 3:21-24 says, "Unto Adam also and to his wife did the LORD God make coats of skins, and clothed them. And the LORD God said, Behold, the man is become as one of us, to know good and evil: and now, lest he put forth his hand, and take also of the tree of life, and eat, and live for ever: Therefore the LORD God sent him forth from the garden of Eden, to till the ground from whence he was taken. So he drove out the man; and he placed at the east of the garden of Eden Cherubims, and a flaming sword which turned every way, to keep the way of the tree of life." From the beginning of time until now, boundaries have been established in the form of the phrase "no" or as the King James Bible says, "shalt not." When man disobeyed God's commands, he entered sin. And since the beginning of time, mankind has had trouble accepting responsibility for his or her own wrongs. This is because we tend to use facts to escape the truth. We'll delve more into that a little later.

If a woman came to you and said, "I left my first husband because he was an abusive cheater," you'd celebrate her for being strong enough to leave, right? If she then said, "I left my second husband because he was a drug-pushing narcissist," what would you say to her? You'd congratulate her for being strong enough to leave him, right? But what if I told you that you are enabling her by doing so? Who's going to check her or correct her for getting in those relationships in the first place? I have a dog that happens to be fairly trained. I often eat my food on a tray table or on my breakfast nook. Even though he can reach the food if he stretched his neck, he knows that food on the table is off limits to him, so whenever I leave a room and there's food on a table, he follows me, not because I've trained him to do this, but because he chooses to do so. I'd like to think that he chooses to remove himself from temptation, rather than to stay there and wrestle with it, but I could be reaching. If I took the food off the table and placed it on the floor, it would be within his reach, and guess what? He'd eat it without waiting for permission. This is because he's learned that anything that's on his level is free-game. Why don't we understand this concept when it comes to dating, marriage, friendships and the like? As a woman, I can say that it's not hard to get a guy. But the kind of guys that are readily available to just about any woman can be compared to the food on the floor. Anybody can have them. They have no boundaries or standards and chances are, they don't respect or acknowledge boundaries. The same is true for women. Any woman who makes herself available to just about any man who asks for her number is fishing at the bottom of the barrel because this is where her self-esteem lies. And if she catches a guy at the bottom, he'll do what bottom-thinkers do. All the same, if she's fishing at the bottom, she'll do what bottom-thinkers do. They rebel. They won't take accountability for their actions. They eventually become professional victims who learn to master the folks at the bottom. Now, don't get me wrong, I'm not using classism to demote or degrade any human being, what I am dealing more so with is what I call a region of thought. Thought regions are just like neighborhoods; some people work hard so they can live in the best of neighborhoods, while some people hate working, so they'll accept whatever they can get for free or as cheap as possible. Your neighborhood of thinking is a reflection of what you've been taking in information-wise, who you've been surrounding yourself with, what you're willing to settle for and what you've allowed to escape the waiting room of your mind and enter into your belief system. Understand that a belief is nothing but an agreement. If you believe God, you agree with Him and therefore, you enter into an agreement with Him. If you don't believe God, you believe Satan by default, and therefore, enter into an agreement with him. In the previous chapter, we discussed the many states of a man. Your agreements are the policies or, better yet, the laws and constitutions of every given state. If you agree with God, for example, in your financial state, He becomes the Head of that state. Consequently, you'll never lack anything for the rest of your life; that is, unless you give His seat away to the enemy.

We all start off in the region of thought that we were raised in. This has nothing to do with your geography. It has everything to do with the mentality you were raised in. Some people had decent parents who raised them to be "normal," and by normal, I mean they fit into societal norms. They weren't too traumatized growing up; they were relatively protected, disciplined and educated. In other words, they didn't stand out from the general public. Some people had great parents who raised them to be "above average." They were incredibly educated, protected and nurtured throughout their many phases of life. Some people had bad parents. They lacked the basic essentials, including correction, protection and information, but this is their normal. Most people raised in bad environments don't see much of anything wrong with their upbringing because it was all they knew. And then, there were some parents who were horrible. They were abusive, neglectful and ignorant. They raised their children lacking everything from information to a healthy, happy, non-toxic environment. And when these children became adults and left home, all they had was what their parents had given them, and some of what they'd learned in school and through their social dealings. This was their region of thought.

Blame Culture and Entitlement

What about our blame culture? In the United States of America, we have a huge problem with blame-shifting and entitlement. As a matter of fact, I dare to say it is a huge part of our culture. I often tell people that one of the ways I got free from the many snares, traps and agreements the enemy had me entangled in was by using a maneuver called accountability. I can't force people to treat me right, but I can choose to heal from every wrong and wound that life impresses upon me. This is because I can choose to forgive people. I've been through many regions of thoughts as I've journeyed towards purpose and out of the pits, ditches and valleys that my ancestors birthed me in and the mud-pits I used to roll around in. I've learned a lot over the years, and while in those seasons, I've endured some really heavy-handed attacks. Many of today's Christians would not survive the hand that was dealt to many of us. I think this is why I passionately hate jealousy, envy, competition, comparison and the like. When someone who's gotten a few paper cuts in life has the audacity to try and sabotage me because of their entitlement, I get frustrated, especially if that person is anointed. *Seriously.* But I can't allow that frustration to ensnare me. Instead, I allow it to motivate me to move on because I know that, in that hour, the enemy has found someone to operate through. Yes, even if they're Christian. Let me rephrase that! Especially if they're Christian!

There are many pits around us; these pits include, but are not limited to the pits of:
1. Entitlement
2. Blame
3. Offense/Unforgiveness
4. Sexual Immorality
5. Complacency
6. Fear
7. Procrastination
8. Comfort (False Peace)
9. Isolation

10. Co-Dependency
11. Ungodly Ambition
12. Worry/Doubt

All of these represent pits or snares, and they are everywhere! In truth, they are bottomless pits, because they have no ending. For example, people who are in unforgiveness will remain there until they choose to come out of it. There's no point nor end to unforgiveness. Satan seduces us into the belief that if someone gets what's due to him or her, that this will satisfy our anger or hurt towards that person. It's not true. It may momentarily appease our anger by inciting another emotion, but the wound will still be there. So, our unforgiveness towards the individual turns into a fact. This simply means that we're not angry with the person anymore, we're just angry—period. And most people won't see this anger until they trip over one of our triggers. This is when we'll feel the weight of the unforgiveness, because it'll take over our thoughts and peace until another event demands our attention. This can take days or sometimes, weeks! And even then, unforgiveness will remain in our hearts until we confront it, reject it and choose to walk in love. Again, all of these issues represent bottomless or endless pits.

In every region of thought, you will have to avoid these snares in the same manner that you avoid stepping into a pothole in the street or falling into a lake. But if you walk with the wrong people or walk with the wrong attitude, it is only a

Your Neighborhood of Thinking

matter of time before you find yourself ensnared. When and if this happens, it is easy to shift the blame to the person or the people who were either walking in front of you (your leaders), walking with you (your peers) or walking behind you (your enemies). But the real trap is blame. You see, the minute you fail to take responsibility for your own choices, even if that choice was keeping the wrong company, you will find yourself having to repeat a season. Why? Because there are certain tools that you need to take from each season in order to survive the next season, and if the filter of your understanding is out of shape, you will process each event in the wrong way. This means, you won't take from the experiences what God intended for you to take from them. Instead, you'll become more fact-focused than you are truth-centered.

- **Fact:** I was married to a man who wrestled with rage and promiscuity.
- **Truth:** I married the man.

Do you see how simple that is?! He had anger issues and issues with monogamy before I even entered the picture, but I completely walked past God's established boundaries to get to him. Please note that the Word of God serves as a boundary! I walked past:

- **2 Corinthians 6:14 (ESV):** Do not be unequally yoked with unbelievers. For what partnership has righteousness with lawlessness? Or what fellowship has light with darkness?
- **Matthew 6:33:** But seek ye first the kingdom of God, and his righteousness; and all these things shall be

added unto you.
- **Romans 12:1:** I appeal to you therefore, brothers, by the mercies of God, to present your bodies as a living sacrifice, holy and acceptable to God, which is your spiritual worship.
- **1 Corinthians 15:33:** Be not deceived: evil communications corrupt good manners.
- **James 4:7:** Submit yourselves therefore to God. Resist the devil, and he will flee from you.

I ran past every boundary that God had established to get to what I wanted. This is why I went through what I'd gone through! It wasn't his fault; it was my own! When God matured me and opened my eyes, I was able to heal and come out of that bubble. Today, I counsel a lot of people, and many of them are stuck in seasons they should have come out of years ago! This is because they can't get past the facts so they can get to the truth! I can tell you all types of horror stories about things I've been through, but I have learned that I am the common denominator in everything that happened to the adult-sized me. This is what maturity looks like! Maturity looks like accountability and if oftentimes feels like stupidity!

Our blame-culture is the reason that people don't understand or respect boundaries. This is why so many believers are bound today. It's easy to see the facts, but it's hard to embrace the truth. Sure, you may have a child with a man who turned out to be a deadbeat father. He may be living a lifestyle contrary to that in which Christ ordained him to live. He may be irresponsible and obnoxious, but the truth is, you had a child with that man. It's that simple. Don't further complicate it. This harsh truth has the power to set you free. Or you may have a child with a woman who turned out to be bitter and vindictive. She may be living a lifestyle that is contrary to the one Christ ordained her to live. She may be double-minded and hateful, but if you hadn't crossed the boundary of God's Word to get to her, you wouldn't be in that predicament. And of course, someone will say, "Well, I'm glad I did do what I did because if I hadn't, I wouldn't have my child!" Who told you that? God is a mysterious God. His thoughts are above our thoughts and His ways are above our ways. Who's to say that you wouldn't be blessed with that very same child someday? The truth is, we don't know! But what we do know is that God is good and He has drawn a boundary around us, and this boundary is called His Word. This is our hedge of protection. God's protective barrier around us isn't some invisible force that covers us while we rebel against Him. No, what covers us when we sin against God is called grace. Anytime we go across a God-established boundary, we enter sin. And while in sin, His grace is sufficient for us, meaning, it's all we need in that season. Of course, he gives us the time, the tools, the space and the doors we need to escape temptation. Needless to say, however, everything that happens to us when we are outside of God's will is our own fault, regardless of how many facts we can extract from those situations. For example, there are sharks in the ocean. We know this. If you jump into the ocean and come across a shark, the shark is not your villain. It's an animal acting on instinct and opportunity. It didn't step out of the water, do a reverse search on your address, come to your house and break in through your bedroom window. You went into its region (the ocean), and unfortunately, it's not human, so it doesn't play by our rules. Take that same concept and apply it to sin. When we go past the boundaries of God's will and into sin, the people who make up that world only do what they instinctively know how to do. God drew those boundaries for a reason, but we chose to cross them, whether it was out of curiosity, ignorance or plain ole rebellion. Either way, we went into sin, met a few folks there, saw their potential, tried to drag them across the borders of righteousness, and eventually, had to drag our battered bodies back into the will of God. Lesson learned; that is, of course, if we forsake the blame culture and just embrace, acknowledge and learn from our mistakes.

We prophesy in part, according to the Bible. This means that we only see a small snippet of what God is doing whenever He chooses to show it to us. Let's say I went to two architectural firms and showed them both sketches of what I want in my future home. I explain to both firms that what I'm showing them is just one of the wings of the house, so I'm not asking them to hire a crew of builders and begin the work just yet. I just want to see a sample blueprint of what that wing could look like. I tell them the property that I'm looking to build on, stopping to mention that:

1. I have not yet purchased the property because the owner listed one acre of land to sell, when he owns the entire five acres. I need the entirety of the land to carry out my plans, but I may have to look elsewhere if he refuses to sell the rest of the land to me.
2. I have to check the city's zoning laws because I'm planning to use the other wing of the house as a professional music studio, meaning, artists can and will pay me to use my equipment, but first, I have to make sure that this is allowed.

Both firms are in competition for my business, and they know this. Being anxious and overly competitive, one of the firms takes it upon themselves to purchase the land that I've been looking at. Of course, they do this without my permission, my signed consent or my knowledge. They manage to talk the seller into selling them two acres. They hire a building crew and immediately get to work. A few months later, I find another piece of property after having learned that the property I was interested in has sold. The new location is even better than the former one. It costs me a little more money, but the amenities, the location and the zoning laws surrounding that property make it all the more worth it. Three days before closing, I receive a call from the other firm. "Your house is ready!" shouts a familiar and excited voice. "What house?" I ask inquisitively, after all, I haven't finalized the blueprint for the house yet. I've found a different firm to draw the house, but now, the blueprint only shows ninety percent of the home. I still haven't approved the left wing yet because I didn't like the drawings my new firm showed me of that particular side, so they went back to the drawing table. The voice on the other end identifies himself as being a contractor with John Doe Architectural Firm. He tells me that they decided to surprise me by buying the property and building the wing of the house I'd shown them months ago. He excitedly tells me that they managed to talk the seller out of two acres and they are hoping that they'll be able to talk him out of more, but if not, they believe they can squeeze my vision into a smaller, more energy-efficient home. I'm devastated, offended and shocked. I explain to the contractor that, for one, I never signed a contract with them, and secondly, I didn't give them the go-ahead to buy that property. That was for me to do. "But ma'am, if you see what we've built, I'm confident you'll love it," says the contractor. "It's a wing, of course, but we'll be able to add on in the near future once we get the seller to sell the rest of the land to us." I let out a loud sigh and say, "I'll meet you there at 3:30 today, but I'm not buying that house from you." The contractor agrees because he's confident that he can change my mind.

At 3:30, I pull up and see a beautiful structure. It looks far better than I imagined, but there's nothing I can do with it. I walk up to the contractor and hand him a letter from the city. It's a letter explaining why that area cannot and will not be zoned as commercial property. I also hand him the blueprint that my new firm has created, explaining to him that I've already purchased another property and that I've already approved ninety percent of the blueprint the other firm has created. I'm simply waiting on them to finish the drawing of the wing before we get started. And lastly, I explain to him that the area I'm moving in is zoned both residential and commercial, meaning, I can build my studio on the property without resistance or delay. The contractor is horrified. "Ma'am, I sure hate that you signed a contract with these guys, but a deal is a deal! We've spent well over two million dollars to complete this project, so it looks like you're about to have two properties. Our administrative department has already emailed you an invoice." Of course, I refuse to pay for the property and the firm ends up taking me to court. It goes without saying that firm loses because I never signed a contract with them. I'd made it clear from the beginning that I was looking at them and another firm to create the blueprint of my vision. I'd gone with another firm and another location. Who's at fault in this? The firm, of course! I showed them a part of the vision; I never told them to start building just yet! Isn't this what we do to God? He shows us a part of the vision, and we start building in the seasons that we're in, not realizing that the vision is of the future. We don't see the fullness of what God has planned because He has not revealed it to us, but we build anyway, thinking that we can force Him to buy into our plans for ourselves. He doesn't. Instead, He leaves us with the bill and urges us to move forward so that we can get the healing and deliverance we'll need to walk into His plans for us. Nevertheless, we insist on staying behind because of the investments we've made. We say, "I've been with my boyfriend for six years! I've given him two babies! I quit school for this guy! I've invested everything that I have into this relationship!" But being the good Father that He is, God still refuses to sign off on that relationship. He allows the people that we've chosen for ourselves to run away; for us women, we can even dare to say that He chased the guys away with our bride prices. He showed them the invoice; He showed them how much growing they would have to do to cover us and how much dying to self they'd have to do to lead us. They took those invoices into consideration, and when it was time to pay up, they went on the run. We then went before God, blaming the guys for our problems and blaming the Lord, Himself, for the destruction of our plans. We're tired of building and having to alienate everything that we've built. We look behind us and see a series of failed relationships (familial, platonic and romantic) that we've spent years doing CPR on before we had no choice but to admit that they were dead. This is what it looks like to build in the wrong season! This is what it looks like to take a prophetic word and attempt to build your entire life around it. And the trap here is blame. One of the lessons we have to learn is that Satan doesn't mind taking the details of a prophetic word and giving us whatever it was that the prophet said! Why? Because Satan is strategic! He knows that it's just a wing or a snippet of what God has for us, and if we accept his offer, we won't readily leave the season that we're in. Wherever we begin to invest, that's where we'll start planting our roots. And if we do start building in the wrong season, we'll likely have to abandon whatever it is that we've built, but the snare of Satan is to get us into blame. Blame

Your Neighborhood of Thinking

chains you to the season that you're in because it does not allow you to get a panoramic view or a bird's-eye view of the situation, event or relationship that God delivered you from. Instead, your position is one-sided or one-dimensional. Your position determines your perspective. Your perspective is your personal interpretation of a situation. A one-dimensional view of a situation is called blame. Blame lists all the facts, but it rarely tells the truth. Facts demand justice, but the truth demands forgiveness. This forgiveness is the product of you admitting that you did something wrong in the first place, even if what you did wrong was the result of good intentions or simply not praying first. Blame is being unwilling to come out of a pit or a ditch without an apology or some form of compensation. It means to forsake your tomorrow because of what happened to you yesterday.

And of course, there are some events that went beyond our control. Let's look at the story of Tamar and her wicked brother, Amnon. Again, 2 Samuel 13:1-19 tells the story. It reads, "Now Absalom, David's son, had a beautiful sister, whose name was Tamar. And after a time Amnon, David's son, loved her. And Amnon was so tormented that he made himself ill because of his sister Tamar, for she was a virgin, and it seemed impossible to Amnon to do anything to her. But Amnon had a friend, whose name was Jonadab, the son of Shimeah, David's brother. And Jonadab was a very crafty man. And he said to him, 'O son of the king, why are you so haggard morning after morning? Will you not tell me?' Amnon said to him, 'I love Tamar, my brother Absalom's sister.' Jonadab said to him, 'Lie down on your bed and pretend to be ill. And when your father comes to see you, say to him, 'Let my sister Tamar come and give me bread to eat, and prepare the food in my sight, that I may see it and eat it from her hand.' So Amnon lay down and pretended to be ill. And when the king came to see him, Amnon said to the king, 'Please let my sister Tamar come and make a couple of cakes in my sight, that I may eat from her hand.' Then David sent home to Tamar, saying, 'Go to your brother Amnon's house and prepare food for him.' So Tamar went to her brother Amnon's house, where he was lying down. And she took dough and kneaded it and made cakes in his sight and baked the cakes. And she took the pan and emptied it out before him, but he refused to eat. And Amnon said, 'Send out everyone from me.' So everyone went out from him. Then Amnon said to Tamar, 'Bring the food into the chamber, that I may eat from your hand.' And Tamar took the cakes she had made and brought them into the chamber to Amnon her brother. But when she brought them near him to eat, he took hold of her and said to her, 'Come, lie with me, my sister.' She answered him, 'No, my brother, do not violate me, for such a thing is not done in Israel; do not do this outrageous thing. As for me, where could I carry my shame? And as for you, you would be as one of the outrageous fools in Israel. Now therefore, please speak to the king, for he will not withhold me from you. But he would not listen to her, and being stronger than she, he violated her and lay with her. Then Amnon hated her with very great hatred, so that the hatred with which he hated her was greater than the love

Your Neighborhood of Thinking

with which he had loved her. And Amnon said to her, 'Get up! Go!' But she said to him, 'No, my brother, for this wrong in sending me away is greater than the other that you did to me.' But he would not listen to her. He called the young man who served him and said, 'Put this woman out of my presence and bolt the door after her.' Now she was wearing a long robe with sleeves, for thus were the virgin daughters of the king dressed. So his servant put her out and bolted the door after her. And Tamar put ashes on her head and tore the long robe that she wore. And she laid her hand on her head and went away, crying aloud as she went."

Tamar hadn't done anything wrong. She'd obeyed her father, and in the process of doing so, she had been raped. Who's to blame in this situation? After all, it is human nature for us to want justice. It is human nature for us to want answers, and we want them both swiftly! The sad truth is, these types of scenarios can and do happen. Who do we blame when our parents or guardians fail to protect us, but instead, are guilty of placing us in harm's way? The answer is—blame the attacker, inform the parent or the guardian and make it a point to heal and forgive. Of course, this is easier said than done! But understand these facts.

- The soul is like clay. It was formed; this is why it can be deformed, conformed and transformed.
- Every season has a particular shape. I'm not talking about geometric shapes such as square, circle, triangle or rectangle. The shape of a season is what we call a belief system.

- Once the soul has been impacted by trauma, it takes on the shape of the attacker. What this means is that the attacker leaves an imprint on the victim's soul. For example, imagine your favorite cartoon character running through a wall and leaving the shape of himself in the space that he impacted. This is what trauma looks like. This opening in the soul allows the attacker to access the subconscious and even impact the unconscious mind at will. This opening serves as an open door for the enemy. Forgiveness closes this door, but unforgiveness sets the stage for more predators to come through that space.

American culture encourages us to hold onto blame. Why is this? First and foremost, consider that fact that America, like most western countries, is a capitalistic nation. Now, if you don't know what capitalism is, Oxford Languages defines it this way "an economic and political system in which a country's trade and industry are controlled by private owners for profit, rather than by the state." In other words, we are a "for profit" nation. We have all types of science and research that backs our medical and political climates, and every commercial climate that funds our government. Please note that most of our research is conducted in college and university laboratories, and this research is funded by the government. Remember, the government is a "for profit" entity that capitalizes off the discoveries made by these agencies. For example, Urology of Virginia reported the following:

> "Last year, the cancer industry was valued at $100 billion, and is predicted to reach $147 billion in sales by 2018, according to data released by the IMS Institute for Healthcare Informatics. The Wall Street Journal recently reported that the average monthly costs for cancer patients now exceed $10,000."
> (Source: Urology of Virginia/Big Pharma earns BILLIONS off cancer drugs/Julie Wilson)

Considering this, why would the government actually want to create a cure for cancer when it makes billions upon billions of dollars off treating the disease? The tobacco industry earns no less than $35 billion dollars a year, and of course, Uncle Sam gets a large chunk of that money, so why would they ban tobacco? The alcohol beverage industry earns on average $70 billion dollars a year, and again, the government profits from this as well. The US Mental Health and Substance Abuse Services industry earns roughly around $50 billion a year. Blame leads to the deterioration of your mental and emotional health. Most people who have issues with forgiveness actually turn to drugs and alcohol. What this means is that the world's system is designed to keep you turned upside down so that it can take as much of your money as possible. This is why it is necessary for you to heal and forgive, and to do this, you have to look deeper into every offense, hurt and rejection that you've suffered through. This is how you come out of victimhood. This is how you forsake the world's system; this is what allows you to:

1. Not make the same mistakes that you've made in the

past.
2. Help others to heal.
3. Learn to generate wealth using your talents, skills and your testimony.

Let's look a little deeper at the state of victimhood.

Victimhood

Again, your region of thought is your neighborhood of thinking. The interesting fact about this is—the human mind is always gathering new information. This is how we advance forward. The more you learn and the more you understand, the more you'll advance. All the same, the more information you reject, the more time you'll spend in a particular region of thought. After a while, should you refuse to learn anything that could advance you forward (not all information is equal), you'll start dealing with what we call cycles. Another word for "cycle" is "stronghold." In other words, you'll stop advancing forward and start going in circles. An example of this behavior is a woman constantly finding herself in non-productive, toxic or abusive relationships. Because she's not gathering new information, she isn't advancing forward; instead, she's learned to master the region of thought she's in. This makes her comfortable with certain types of men. In other words, she has a comfort zone, and she's unwilling to leave it, even if her life is at risk. As a matter of fact, because she's so love-starved, she's developed a way to get attention, and that is by casting herself as a victim. And while this may sound heartless, the truth is, she's not a victim. I'm a victim if her lover runs up to me and starts hitting me, only

Your Neighborhood of Thinking

because I don't know him. But for her, she's not a victim. She's a willing participant in her own destruction; that is, unless, she's TRULY trying to break free, but is being held against her will. If she's there because she has hope that her man will change, she's not a victim. (The misuse of this word is stopping people who are truly victims from getting the help that they need.) The term "victim" has an expiration date attached to it. You can only be a victim but for so long. After a while, you're no longer a victim; instead, you're just toxic, but you may be getting the worst end of that toxic relationship. Anytime a person refuses to come out of a region of thought, that person will master that region. The mastermind of any given region of thought is called a manipulator. If you've ever tried to help someone out of a bad situation who has been casting himself or herself as a victim, you soon learned that the person had no intention of leaving that situation. Instead, they used you:

1. For money
2. For sympathy
3. For a place to stay
4. For a shoulder to cry on
5. To scare, intimidate or provoke the person or people they claim are preying on them (an example of this is a woman saying to her abusive lover, "That's okay! There's a woman named Jane who's offered to let me live in her house if you don't straighten up and get your act together!")

And to be fair, there are some women who are victims of

their abusers; they have not yet left those relationships because the men in their lives are holding them hostage, either by threatening to kill them, threatening their children, threatening their families or using some other fear tactics. But having once been what the world would call a victim of abuse, I learned that only the desperate get free, and in order to become desperate, you have to stop thinking like a victim. In other words, you have to come outside a particular region of thought, and to do this, you may need the help of others. All the same, you have to be willing to receive that help. For example, I'd found myself sitting on the witness stand, trying with everything in me to keep from crying. The judge was an African American woman with dreadlocks. She had the face of a loving, but strict mother. I was trying to get the restraining order extended that I'd gotten against the man I was in the process of divorcing. She'd just berated him for his abusive ways and now, it was my turn to hear her hard words of wisdom. I don't cry easily, but that day, I could feel that oh-so-familiar lump in my throat and I fought it with everything in me. After a few hard, but loving words, she told me about a program for women who had been the victims of domestic violence. *Victim?* That word bothered me so much! But the crazy part is, that's how the enemy had managed to keep me in that predicament for so long. I refused to acknowledge that I was not in control. For me, the idea of sitting in a room with a bunch of ex-girlfriends and ex-wives, sharing stories about abuse sounded like nothing more than a bitterness fest, and I wanted no part of it. Somehow, the judge could tell that I wasn't receiving her words all too well, so she softened her voice a little more and continued to urge me to go to those meetings. She could see that I was a broken vessel, so as strict as she was (I'd sat in some of her proceedings before), she'd chosen to handle me with kid gloves, and of course, this is what put enough pressure on my emotions so that I could begin to grieve, not just that relationship, but the mentality I had. Needless to say, I never went to a single domestic violence meeting because what I didn't realize at that time was that she was offering me new information. My perception was off. All I could think of was having to tell my story to a bunch of women who I didn't know. What would they do with that information? Would they gossip about me? Would they judge me? Would they use that information to embarrass me? What if they knew someone who I knew and they shared my story with that person? I had already started cutting off a bunch of messy kin-folks who loved gossip, and because of my experiences with them, I was not about to share "my business" with a bunch of strangers. Again, this is how I saw it, and because of that mindset, I remained in the victim mentality for longer than I should have.

There are different types of people with victim mentalities. They are:
1. **Attention-Seekers:** These people love the attention they get whenever they play the victim. They are always entering toxic relationships, and they love the attention they get from people outside the relationship when they share photos of themselves with black

Your Neighborhood of Thinking

eyes, busted lips and bruises. When their abusers finally leave them, attention-seekers will always find someone else to be the victims of, including friends. For example, if you ever correct or begin to distance yourself from an attention-seeker, that person will cast you as a villain, all the while, casting himself or herself as a victim of your tyrannical ways. They refuse to be in healthy relationships. As a matter of fact, if you introduce them to good, wholesome, God-fearing people, they will mishandle, reject or abuse those folks! These broken souls love to post photos of themselves in hospital beds, and if someone they know gets sick, they'll come to the hospital ready to take a picture of themselves standing alongside that person so they can post it to social media. They will use, for example, the fact that their uncle had pancreatic surgery as a way to draw attention to themselves. They love sympathy, and whenever they do get sick or wounded, they see their issue as an opportunity to shine. They'll go live on social media to talk about their issues, and you can see the joy in their eyes as they read the live comments from the people who are feeding them with the attention they so hunger for.

2. **Self-Seekers:** These people are like grenades. They are bad people who go into bad situations with seemingly good intentions. These characters are very subtle! And the amazing part about this particular group of victims is that many of them will date and

marry a toxic person with every intention of doing right by that person, but deep down within the core of their being lies a very strategic and deceptive spirit. That spirit lies and waits for an opportunity to draw attention to itself. It is the spirit of pride, witchcraft and accusation. For example, a self-seeking man will marry a woman who has a reputation for being promiscuous, dishonest or sneaky. He'll then do great and marvelous things for her—publicly! Everyone who knows the couple will talk about how much that man loves and spoils his wife! And everyone who knows the couple will talk about how rotten and undeserving his wife is! This allows him to garner the sympathy and attention that he wants. He's just as predatory as she is, but because he doesn't have extramarital affairs and because he's somewhat docile, he's often seen as the victim. In most cases, he's the most wicked one in the relationship, but he hides his evil ways behind soft-spoken words and kind gestures. Howbeit, if you were to live in their home, you'd see him provoking his wife by watching porn, behaving questionably around her daughters and in many cases, downright ignoring and neglecting his wife. All the same, a self-seeking woman will marry a man who has a reputation for having anger issues or being downright wicked. She'll do (what appears to be) all the right things for him, and you'll notice that he responds angrily. This makes her appear to be a docile, sweet and harmless soul, while he appears to be nothing less than a monster. But if you watch them closely, you'll notice the little things that she does to provoke him. For example, if the couple were to go to a cookout, the woman would get up and help prepare the food; she'll even prepare a plate for him and be extremely kind. You may see him behaving angrily towards her, but if you pay attention to her movements, you'll also see her pulling a bunch of disappearing acts. For example, she'll volunteer to go to the store to buy bread. If her husband talks about going with her, she'll insist that he stays behind, promising that she'll be right back. The store in this example is five minutes away, and it's a small convenience store that never has a lot of customers. This lady will be gone for an hour and a half, and whenever her husband calls her, she won't answer his calls or she'll switch her phone off. By the time she comes back, her husband will be scared, angry and suspicious, and because he's emotional and unstable, he may create a scene at the cookout. This makes him appear to be predatory and her appear to be a sweet and harmless woman in a bad situation. Or on a lighter note, she'll steal away to an empty bedroom with another guy and claim to have been encouraging him. People who have this spirit will join a church, movement or mentorship and seemingly do all the right things, but in the background, they'll move dishonorably. It's hard for a leader to correct this person because on the forefront, the person appears

Your Neighborhood of Thinking

to be honorable and helpful, but the person may be creating relationships with other members and then, engaging in subtle gossip. The person is setting the stage for the spirit of accusation, and whenever his or her movements are brought under scrutiny, the person will cast himself or herself as a victim, leaving the church and retreating into a cave. Understand that soul ties are like magnets; the goal or assignment of that person was to create relationships within that church and then leave, taking a few members with himself or herself.

3. **Co-Dependents:** Co-dependents are people bound by the Ahab spirit. They hate responsibility. They want someone to take physical custody and care of them or, at minimum, handle every issue and person that serves as a weight in their lives. They'll stay in toxic situations, not because they have to, but because they don't want to take care of themselves. They will complain about their offenders, but will not leave these people for too long. Again, this is because their offenders are also their providers (parents, boyfriends, girlfriends, spouses, friends, etc.). Whenever I'm counseling this category of people, I often challenge them to see if they truly want to be free or if they simply want to relieve themselves by talking about the situation. I will normally say something like, "Okay. Just move out and get your own place." When you start talking like that to someone in this category, that person will stop calling you because again, he or she

doesn't want to be free. That person just wants to gripe. Co-dependents are often paired with narcissists. Another word for narcissist is the Jezebel spirit.
4. **Master Manipulators:** These are the people who've mastered a particular region of thought, and they have learned to work the system in that region. For example, I once knew a woman who was in an abusive relationship. I was young and naive, so I pitied her and despised her boyfriend. She got people to pity her and she used that pity to cover her indiscretions. Like most people, I eventually came to realize that she was a serial-cheater, and while this does not and cannot justify her boyfriend's choice to abuse her, I soon learned that his abuse played into some sick fairy tale she had going in her head. She correlated abuse with love, and she did a lot of things to provoke him. She was also an attention-seeker, so she would use the fact that he'd hit her to get sympathy from others. Master manipulators say what you want to hear in order for them to get what they want from you. They are skilled actors who will cry or threaten to take their own lives in order to get from you whatever it is that they want, whether it be your attention, some money, a place to stay, etc.
5. **Idolaters:** These souls worship the people who serve as predators in their lives. They'd rather die than to live without these people. People in this category offer many sacrifices to whomever or whatever it is that

they want. Their children are even on this list! For example, a woman in this category would ask her boyfriend of one month to babysit her three-year old daughter while she goes to work. She puts her daughter at risk so that she can prove to the man that nothing she has is off limits to him. Now, she may not want the guy to touch her daughter inappropriately, but she's willing to take that risk in order for her to win favor with that man. Idolaters will talk about the abuse they've endured, but they will not leave their abusers! As a matter of fact, if you happen to be around when their lovers attack them and you jump into this fight, an idolater will turn around and start fighting you. They offer their children, their families, their friends and their pastors as sacrifices, meaning, they will sacrifice those relationships, and then go and brag to their idols about ending those relationships. They do this in hopes that the men and women they idolize will see their sacrificial offerings as tokens of their love, and that by doing this, they'll prove how serious they are about the relationships. They love to talk about their relationships, readily sharing details of their lovers' insecurities, abusive tendencies and questionable behaviors, but they don't do this because they want their self-esteem built up. They don't do this because they are hurting. They do this because they are looking for something to sacrifice to their lovers. For example, the minute you tell them that they can do better or that their lovers are clearly not that into them, they will often respond by being argumentative or by getting off the phone with you. They will then tell their lovers four things: how relevant you are or were in their lives, how long you've been a part of their lives, what you said to them, and lastly, how they responded to your "interference." Again, this is done to make the object of their affections feel more secure and to prove to their lovers that they are serious about the relationship. They will even evict their own children! This is especially true if their relationships appear to be in danger, for example, if their lovers are entertaining romantic relationships with other people.

6. **Dreamers:** Also known as hopeless romantics, these people are more in love with their fantasies than they are with their lovers. They've watched one too many romance comedies, and every person who romantically engages this category of victims is also immediately drafted into a series of fantasies that they've been having. Like idolaters, they "fall" in love way too fast and they almost always introduce some type of villain into their relationships just so the two of them can have something to overcome together. But unlike idolaters, they aren't necessarily willing to sacrifice people who are important to them. Instead, they'll focus on their lovers' exes or anyone who is actually interfering with their relationships or with their lovers. For example, if the man that a woman is engaging romantically has an upcoming court date

Your Neighborhood of Thinking

with his former bosses, the dreamer will readily and actively insert herself into the fight. She will help the guy to gather evidence, suggest a few defenses and even offer to pay some or all of the guy's legal fees. The great thing about dreamers, however, is that they eventually do wake up and realize that they are wasting their time, even though they may sleep and slumber for years. The bad thing about them is, like everyone else on this list, they have trouble accepting the fact that they are the common denominators in their own hurt.

The victim mentality keeps people from advancing forward because they always have some unfinished business that needs to be tended to. Think of it this way. A woman who lives in Chicago, Illinois ends up moving to Atlanta, Georgia, but she has a court date in three months in Chicago. This is unfinished business, so even though she's moved on, she still has to return to the place that she left. And while this may work in the physical realm, anytime you leave a region of thought, you can't simply return to it because of unfinished business. As a matter of fact, the door to your next season won't open until you resolve the issues in the season that you're in right now. In other words, you will never leave one season and enter the next if you're hosting a victim's mentality.

Something else that's worth being noted is this—if you'll notice, most of the women who've been killed by their husbands actually escaped those men at one point in their lives, but for whatever reason, they'd returned to those relationships. I've shared this with countless women who were serving as victims of abuse, warning them that you cannot and should never have a revolving door in a relationship. If you're going to be in it, stay there. If you're going to leave, don't go back! Why is it that a man can kill a woman who's left him before? It's simple. Because he's experienced life without her, and it was hell to him! He's experienced relationships with other women, but none of them could compare to her! So, when she returned to the relationship, he didn't just embrace her, he tightened his grip on her. He reasoned within himself that he could not live without her, but seeing that she was able to live without him is tormenting to him. This is especially true if she had been successful outside of their relationship. The point is, the minute she returned to that relationship, he'd decided that the only way out from that point on was death! Demons think the same way! Again, Matthew 12:43-45 says, "When the unclean spirit has gone out of a person, it passes through waterless places seeking rest, but finds none. Then it says, 'I will return to my house from which I came.' And when it comes, it finds the house empty, swept, and put in order. Then it goes and brings with it seven other spirits more evil than itself, and they enter and dwell there, and the last state of that person is worse than the first." If a devil is cast out, but the person doesn't change the key (point of access), that spirit will return, but this time, it will go out of its way to ensure that it won't be cast out again! The message here is once you leave a region of thought, you must absolutely commit within your own heart that you won't return to it UNLESS God sends you back to recover others. I can legally reenter some regions of thought that I've escaped, but I can't go there to make friends. My assignment is to bring people up and out! But I could not and would not have escaped those regions if I thought of myself as a victim! I've been betrayed in every region of thought, I've been rejected in every region of thought, I've been abandoned in every region of thought, I've been mishandled in every region of thought and I've been overlooked in every region of thought, but these were just some of the obstacles along the way. The goal wasn't for me to take to social media and talk about my "haters." This is where so many people get stuck! These obstacles could either fuel me or fool me; the choice was my own! Like most people, I stood behind some of these obstacles for days, weeks, months and even years, trying to understand why I'd been dealt that particular hand. But as I began to mature, I learned to maneuver myself around those barriers by forgiving folks, praying for them and just blessing them whenever I could. This wasn't an easy feat, but through prayer and guidance, I managed to get by those obstacles, heal and move on! I refused to call myself a victim; instead, I learned that I am more than a conqueror through Christ Jesus, and while this may sound poetic, it simply means that I entered a fixed fight and didn't have to move a muscle! Christ overcame Satan on my behalf!

Remember, you can't turn to the system to help you

overcome your demons. God designed us to navigate from one state of mind to another, but this journey is not an easy one. It requires that we:
1. Study and show ourselves approved for the next level.
2. Heal.
3. Forgive.
4. Help others.
5. Guard our hearts.
6. Move on!

By doing this, we will slowly but surely arrive at the peak of our purpose. Apostle Paul said it this way, "I press toward the mark for the prize of the high calling of God in Christ Jesus." Read this carefully—Satan is terrified of a believer who will face off with him in every season, refusing to quit or feel sorry for himself or herself! This is how we die to ourselves; this is what renders Satan ineffectual in our lives because, over time, we'll begin to see the light of our own personal Promised Lands, meaning, we'll begin to emerge from the wilderness of victimhood and enter into our purpose. Please note that your assignment or the reason God birthed you in the Earth is the place where you'll find the most peace; this is the neighborhood of thinking that Satan is working nonstop to keep you out of!

UNDERSTANDING REJECTION

In every region of thought, you will find what we refer to as cliques. Merriam Webster defines the word "clique" as: "a narrow exclusive circle or group of persons especially: one held together by common interests, views, or purposes." In any social environment, you'll see cliques; you'll see groups of people pooling together, and you'll notice that they tend to come together exclusively anytime they are in the same proximity. Cliques are often relatively exclusive gatherings for people with shared interests or beliefs. And while it is easy to feel left out, rejected or judged by a clique, you have to understand how God works. While we see this clotting or coming together of souls, what we don't see are the invisible lines that separate them from us; these lines or boundaries can be good, they can be bad or they can be perceived. Either way, they represent mindsets. A mindset is whatever a person has set his or her mind to. It's the coming together of beliefs, theories, perspectives and plans that the person has embraced. When a group of people come together, it is oftentimes because they have set their minds to the same things. It is important to note that every clique is a body; it has a head and a brain, just as it has members. The head or brain (leader) of any given clique determines the overall mindset and climate of that group. So, if the head of a clique is a promiscuous, but religious woman who passionately hates Christian men, the other women, whether they agree with her position or not, will have to follow suit. In other words, they will have to mirror her belief system. Now, they don't have to necessarily agree with her in regards to men, sex or relationships, but they have to have a common or shared interest somewhere. This is what allows them to remain connected. This is the soul tie between them. All the same, all cliques aren't bad. There can be a clique of women who are relatively good people with good intentions, but again, every clique has a head; this is the authority of that clique, and that person will determine how far each individual within that setting can go. She can't stop the people from growing, but if a member of that group goes or grows beyond her understanding or what she's comfortable with, she can and may respond in a negative way. To her, a person who grows past her or goes beyond her realm of understanding may appear to be a competitor and someone who cannot be trusted. She may reflect on the countless people who've walked out of her life, for example, after having gotten a college degree or accomplished some small or great feat. Consequently, she may remove you from that clique. In doing so, she doesn't necessarily have to speak evil of you to the members. Because the members of that group follow her, they will notice, for example, if she is no longer engaging with you or speaking to you. They will notice how she responds to questions about you and they will follow suit. This is because they are members (workers, followers) and not heads (thinkers) of that particular group. It's important and necessary for everyone, especially leaders, pioneers and generational curse-breakers to know

Understanding Rejection

that these women and men <u>are not</u> villains but can become villains if you are a part of their network and you attempt to grow beyond their scope of reasoning. Honestly, because rejection hurts so badly and makes us self-conscious about our own shortcomings, we oftentimes get angry at the folks who rejected us or the people we feel are rejecting us. We do this because WE LACK UNDERSTANDING! Let me explain.

Let's say that you have a daughter who's smart, ambitious and bold. She's 17-years old and about to enter her last year of high school. One day, she brings home a new friend by the name of Mandy. Mandy is nice, but she's not ambitious at all. She has a boyfriend, so she's decided to put off college, get married and work from home while her husband goes to work with his father. But your daughter is a genius and you don't want her following in Mandy's footsteps. Your frustration and worries are intensified once you realize that Mandy has what we call an "alpha" personality, meaning, she doesn't submit to anyone. She absolutely, unequivocally has to be the leader of every relationship she enters, including friendships. This tells you that your daughter will be a member of Mandy's clique (and not the other way around), whether that clique includes two people or twelve people. But again, Mandy is truly a nice young lady. She's helpful, respectable and very protective of your daughter. So, later on that day, you make the tough decision to speak with your daughter after Mandy has left. You explain to her that you don't want her around Mandy, and of course, she doesn't

Understanding Rejection

take this very well. You try to help her to understand your reasoning, but no matter what you say, you sound like the villain to her, so you decide to be quiet and let her learn on her own through an event called experience. Experience is wisdom's belt carrier; it is the disciplinarian that God uses to sober us up. So, for the remainder of their senior year, your daughter and Mandy are pretty much inseparable. Like Mandy, your daughter gets herself a boyfriend and Mandy tries to convince her that she should consider marrying her beau, and then, head off to college a year or so later. As hard as it is for you to stand on the sidelines and watch your daughter face the temptation that is Mandy, you resolve within yourself to just be prayerful and give your daughter the tools, information and the affirmation she needs to keep growing. A few days before her graduation, your daughter breaks up with her boyfriend because she's discovered that he's been entertaining other girls, and Mandy is livid. She comes over to your home and you overhear her demanding that your daughter forgive her beau; she constantly reiterates that the girl your daughter caught him with is known for being flirtatious and promiscuous. She says that she knows where the girl works, and suggests that your daughter goes to the girl's job to confront her. Of course, Mandy plans to be there as well. You utilize that moment to walk into the kitchen where the girls are talking and offer Mandy some wisdom. You say to her, "Mandy, I raised Natalie to first love and respect herself. If Fred is cheating on her now, it's not going to get better; it's only going to get worse, especially since he's only 18-years old. Men can come and most will go, but no one can take your education away from you. I didn't raise Natalie to put all of her trust in a man. I raised her to put her trust in God and to get an education. I didn't raise Natalie to fight over a man. I raised her to be better than that. I respect her wishes; this is why I try to give her space and the freedom to make her own mistakes, but what I cannot and will not do is sit on the sidelines in my own home while you push her towards a relationship that both you and I know is unhealthy for her. I want what's best for you as well. You should consider college before marriage, but that's your choice. It's not Natalie's choice; it's yours. She won't be any less of a friend if she makes a different choice than you do." Of course, your daughter is a little bothered by your interruption, but she gets over it. Ultimately, she makes the right decision; she chooses to go to one of the colleges that offered her a scholarship.

While at college, Natalie makes some new friends, and even though she tries to remain in contact with Mandy, Mandy stops answering her calls. During spring break, your daughter comes home from college, and almost immediately, she goes to visit the newly married Mandy, but Mandy doesn't open her door. She sees Mandy at the mall walking with her new friends, but when she approaches the women, Mandy treats her like a stranger. Natalie is hurt and she feels rejected. Is Mandy a villain? No. Are her friends villains? Nope. They are the pillars of a region of thought; in other words, they live within a certain neighborhood of thinking and reasoning. When Natalie decided to move out of that neighborhood, what she didn't realize was that she could no longer be led by Mandy. Mandy could no longer be the head in their relationship. Now, this doesn't mean that Natalie would be the head; it simply means that the relationship would have to be redefined. Mandy has an alpha-personality; she doesn't want to be a part of anything that she isn't in headship over because she fears losing control. Natalie may be wounded in the platonic state because of this event, but if you give her the information she needs to heal, she should make a full recovery. Mandy, on the other hand, may turn out to be an awesome friend to the women in her circle for the rest of their lives. Her inability to maintain a friendship with your daughter is not necessarily a reflection of her character. It is a reflection of her lack of knowledge, her fears and her unwillingness to learn how to have relationships that don't mirror the ones she's used to having. Believe it or not, this is a very common problem. As a matter of fact, I dare to say that more than ninety percent of humans don't know how to have relationships with people who they can't relate to; this is why they tend to pool or congregate into cliques. And again, the members of a clique are not always villains. Most of the time, they simply fear letting new people into their circles, especially people who have alpha-like tendencies. In other words, no organization or creature can have two heads. So, they may be wise in not allowing you to be a part of what they've built if they feel that you are a threat to the structure of it. Again, it can and does feel bad, especially for those of us who are builders. We face rejection a LOT, and we have to acclimate ourselves to it so that we aren't negatively impacted by it.

Next, every clique has a capacity. This capacity is determined by the head or, better yet, the thinker of that particular group. Think about a church building. It has a capacity. The same is true of an elevator or any place where people gather. If the head of a clique is an introvert, chances are, the clique will be comprised of two to five people, depending on his or her capacity. If the head of a clique is an extrovert, chances are, the clique will be comprised of six or more people. If the head of a clique is an ambivert, chances are, the person will have several cliques in one or more settings. For example, in any given workplace, you'll see a clique of about three women, with the loudest one being the head of that particular clique. You may also notice that the leader is a part of another clique in that particular workplace where she is either the head or a member. What's amazing is, she will strategically keep these cliques apart in order to maintain her headship over her clique; this is because she may admire the head of another clique, but want to maintain the climate or honor system of the clique she heads. So, if she attempted to merge those cliques, the people who follow her would probably start following the head of the clique that she's a member of. But again, every clique has a capacity. Most of them are comprised of three to five people, and while the leaders of each clique may associate with other people, she will not invite more than three to five people on an outing.

Understanding Rejection

I remember asking God why some leaders couldn't seem to grow their congregations, for example, they may have 30 members at any given time, but they can never seem to rise above the number 30. Every time a new family enters their churches, another family leaves. And this cycle has been playing out for years; sometimes decades! The Lord responded and pretty much told me that this represented their capacity to love others. You see, you can't lead a large group of people if you don't have enough love to cover them. God won't put more on us than we can bear; we've all heard this and it is true. The same is true for cliques. Some people can't handle having 12 friends because they don't know how to say no. Their friends would consume their time and their resources. Others don't have the capacity to love more than five friends because they are too fragile and self-centered to keep up with that many people. This is to say that a clique is a small congregation; yes, even the cliques that pool around one another in your local assemblies. They are congregations within congregations, complete with a leader and members. The leader of a clique won't necessarily refer to himself or herself as the leader; this is pretty much assumed and understood within their group. All the same, everyone on the outside can tell who the leader is because of their body language, the way they position themselves when they stand together and the order in which they walk. The alpha male or female will almost always be at the center whenever they congregate together and will almost always walk just slightly ahead of the rest. The people within the clique will instinctively walk just a step or more behind, and if

Understanding Rejection

they ever start walking ahead of the clique's leader, the members and the leader of that group will start to experience offense. This is because that member has crossed a boundary, and just like any organization, there are members within a clique who desire to be the center of attention. In other words, they want the leader's role, so they will challenge the alpha male or female by:
1. Gossiping about or slandering the leader of that clique to one or more of the members.
2. Flirting, stealing or sleeping with the leader's boyfriend or girlfriend.
3. Walking ahead of that leader or suddenly switching directions whenever the group is walking together.
4. Openly challenging the leader in front of the other members.
5. Starting their own clique within that clique or starting one outside of it.

But why are we talking about cliques? What does this have to do with boundaries? It's simple. Most of the seasons that we get stuck in is because of rejection. And if we come to understand the invisible lines, plus, the settings of any given clique, we will learn how to move effortlessly from one region of thought or season to another. You see, most people who are stuck in a particular mindset are stuck there because they are still slaves of the systems that those mindsets are built on. For example, many Americans who are thirty-years old and older have not yet escaped the systems that were set up in the high schools they attended. They still go by their high school nicknames, they're still mad at the folks who rejected them back then and they are still talking about some of the highlights of their high school tenures. But if they understood that they weren't rejected or overlooked, but instead, God strategically kept them from being a part of an organization that was on the verge of climaxing or collapsing, they would be able to move on. How can they move on? By letting go of the past so they'll have the capacity to embrace their futures.

Shallow. Think about what that word truly means. Merriam Webster's Online Dictionary defines the word "shallow" as "having little depth." I've pretty much been friends with just about every type of personality alive. One of my former "cliques" used to always accuse me of bringing in strays. Yes, this was the actual terminology they used. In it, they meant that I was befriending everyone and inviting them into our circle. They didn't like this. I didn't understand the laws and rules that govern cliques at that time, so I thought the goal was to grow the group. So, anytime I came across someone I thought was cool, I would invite that person to hang out with us. And this offended my friends. Looking back, I can truly say that it took me years to understand how cliques worked. I just thought my friends were shallow, and I spent many years fussing at them about it. This is why they called me "Mamma." As God has brought me through the heights and the depths of this event we call life, I've met many people, from the beautiful, popular and entitled girl to the girl who could've, should've and would've gotten 25 years to life if God had waited one more day to step into her situation. I've had rich friends, I've had poor friends, I've had American friends and I've had foreign friends. For me, I've always been curious about the different types of people and what makes them tick. And throughout many of those relationships, I found that most of those women and men were shallow. The beautiful, popular and entitled girl felt like life owed her the best of the best without any effort or sacrifice on her part. She believed that her beauty qualified her for the handsome, debonair, wealthy, Instagram-famous guy. Doors opened for her, but her entitlement caused those doors to shut violently and abruptly in her face. The not-so-popular girl who had been rejected because of one of the many "isms" of life (I'll describe shortly), on the other hand, felt entitled to an explanation and an apology, not just from her peers and her parents, but from God. She lived her life as a victim, always blaming everyone for her pain and her failures. Which of these two women are more shallow? Neither. They're equally shallow, meaning, they lack depth. In other words, they didn't go beyond the obvious. For the beautiful, popular lady, her looks became her stronghold. For the not-so-beautiful lady, her looks became her stronghold. Either way, both women were being held captive by their own reflections. They didn't search beyond what they could clearly see, what they felt or what they'd experienced. And both lost out on a lot because they lacked depth.

In meeting with the many personality types, I learned that every woman has insecurities and every woman has fears. I remember having a close friend who was absolutely, breathtakingly gorgeous. She was a very humble woman, even though a lot of the women in our workplace didn't like her. As a matter of fact, the "clique" I was a part of didn't like her because she laughed loudly, was super girly, and to be honest, she didn't always respond when people spoke to her. My other friends were gorgeous as well, but they were more "down to Earth" and worldly than she was. They partied, drank and lived life on the edge. But this particular friend was more reserved, classy and soft-spoken. We'll call her "Asia." Of course, I had a separate friendship with Asia than I did with the clique. I remember walking up on Asia at work one day, and I noticed that she was crying. Of course, I went over to her to see what was wrong, and after a few minutes, she finally responded by pointing to her face. She looked up at me and said something I'll probably never forget. She referred to her beauty as a curse. Asia and I were different types of souls. For me, if I came across a woman who wrestled with jealousy, I would provoke her jealousy all the more. I wouldn't speak to her; instead, I would pass her by as if she didn't exist. If she looked at me and scoffed, I would giggle, put my head in the air, pop my lips and strut pridefully right past her. In other words, I would try to provoke her. Her rejection would provoke my rejection, and we'd engage in a silent war of egos. But Asia was a relatively innocent soul. I asked her why she referred to her beauty as a curse, and she said that women judged her the minute she walked into a room. She said that half of the women in our workplace didn't speak to her, and she didn't understand why they

Understanding Rejection

hated her. Of course, I gave her some bad advice. I told her how I tormented those types of women, but this wasn't the route she wanted to take. All the same, I've had friends who weren't so attractive (by society's standards), and they've never actually said it out loud, but many of them saw their faces as curses. They thought that women who were more socially accepted had easier lives, and I had to break it to them that this simply wasn't true. Asia, like many of these women, soon learned that she wasn't just being rejected because of how she looked, she was being rejected because she was simply passing through a region of thought, one that she would ultimately escape. She was also being rejected, in some cases, because she played into people's perceptions of her by not always responding whenever they spoke to her. After being her friend for a while, I learned that this wasn't a pride thing; she simply would zone out or be so deep in her own thoughts that she wouldn't hear the people around her at times. This is because she would sometimes have a lot on her mind. She ended up getting promoted, and like Esther, her beauty opened doors for her, but her humility kept them open. Some of the friends who accused me of bringing in strays, however, did not fair well in this event we call life. They were beautiful, smart and they could have moved mountains if they'd chosen to, but many of them got stuck because they kept recycling old information. I've learned that beauty or the lack thereof doesn't get anyone anywhere. Information does. Humility does. And more than anything, surrendering to God takes us further than any relationship, any job or any platform could ever take us. Asia wanted to fit in, but that wasn't the space for her to fit into, and get this—where there is no space for you, there will be no grace for you. God's grace will cover you, but man's grace will expose you.

Sometimes, God won't allow you to "fit in" because your time in that region of thought is short-lived. You'll meet people who are similar to you (in some cases), and you'll be able to walk with them as long as you're in their mental zip code or their regions of thought. But eventually, you won't be able to relate to them anymore. Please note that a region of thought is also called a season. A season is not solely a time-span or a time-stamped event; it is a pocket of information or, better yet, a set of beliefs, expectations and goals that have merged together within a window of time to create your reality. The time factor of a season is called grace. This is the space or the time that God extends to us to complete an assignment. The set of beliefs or information in any given season has three layers to it. They are: knowledge, understanding and wisdom. All of these layers serve as steps, and once we reach the top or pinnacle of that particular season, we're able to exit it. Knowledge is the foundation. It is the information that we take in, but remember, information goes directly to the waiting room of the soul. This means that true knowledge is powerless until it has been accepted as truth. Once that knowledge goes into the subconscious, it is broken down into understanding. Understanding is needed to explain what we've learned to others. That information will begin to burrow itself; it'll dig

Understanding Rejection

until it reaches the unconscious. This is the light of the soul; this is the most important structure of the human. This is the person's spirit! Once knowledge has become understanding and dug its way to the third level, it becomes wisdom. This means that it become instinctual for the person. It's integrated itself, not just into the person's belief system, but it has become a part of the person. These beliefs, expectations and goals, once they've entered the subconscious, create a magnetic field around you, attracting people who are similar to you and repelling people who cannot relate to you. Many of the people you'll meet have something that may be beneficial to where you're going, and you have to humble yourself in order to receive whatever it is that they have to offer. The caveat is—these people are oftentimes folks you can't relate to and don't want to relate to. They may not fit into your fantasy of the future; they may not look or sound like the folks you want in your circle, and your rejection of them could be crippling to your advancement. This is why we have to be consistent in our prayer lives and humble enough to not only receive an answer from God, but to accept that answer. Some of the most impactful people I've had in my life were folks I would never have picked for myself! For example, the clique of friends I had presented a new experience for me. They were nothing like my high school friends. I learned a lot, both good and bad, from them. Asia was definitely someone I wouldn't have ever befriended on my own. She'd approached me after hearing my friends gossiping about me. I soon learned that she truly had a beautiful spirit, and she opened my eyes to another world, another reality and another set of beliefs. In truth, after meeting and befriending Asia, I no longer prejudged anyone. I learned to embrace different types of people. I also realized that I was right in wanting to get to know people; my clique of friends were just limited in their views, and this is okay! This is just where they were at the time.

In every one of these pockets or seasons, there are people who have climaxed and settled down; they are at the peak of their success. And when you come across them, they are the celebrities or the most celebrated people within those bubbles or circles. You may desire to fit in with them and the people who make up their cliques, but if this is not the peak of what God has called you to, you will often experience rejection unless you beat your soul into place in a process called conformation. Conformation is a largely accepted form of deformation.

Rejection isn't always blatant; sometimes, it's sensed. But again, this rejection isn't always as malicious as we perceive it to be. It's just God's way of keeping us from conforming and peaking in the wrong season or accepting a role that is contrary to the one He's assigned us to. For example, think about high school. In most high schools, there were a group of girls who were at the peak of their success. They were popular, pretty and oftentimes arrogant. For all intents and purposes, we were all sure that they would be successful in this event we call life. So, they were admired and oftentimes

Understanding Rejection

favored while in high school. Then again, they were very particular about who they allowed in their circles. For the most part, they would strategically surround themselves with other young ladies using one of the five "isms". They used racism, classism, lookism, colorism or materialism as their guides. The suffix "ism" denotes a discriminatory practice. Let's look at each word individually to get a better understanding. Please note that the following definitions were taken from Merriam Webster:

- **Racism:** racial prejudice or discrimination
- **Classism:** prejudice or discrimination based on class
- **Lookism:** prejudice or discrimination based on physical appearance and especially physical appearance believed to fall short of societal notions of beauty
- **Colorism:** prejudice or discrimination especially within a racial or ethnic group favoring people with lighter skin over those with darker skin
- **Materialism:** a preoccupation with or stress upon material rather than intellectual or spiritual things

Note: Anytime a clique is formed inside of an "ism," that clique has climaxed or is on the verge of peaking! You can never escape a season unless you give up the throne you sit on and the crown you've worn in that particular season. I've lived long enough to state this as a fact! This is because God won't back this behavior, after all, the suffix "ism" means: "an oppressive and especially discriminatory attitude or belief." Remember, a season is nothing but a mindset or a belief system within a pocket of time! This is why arrogant men and women who use their flesh to get ahead don't go very far in life!

Let's revisit the topic of high school cliques. In every one of these cliques, there was a head; she was often referred to as the "queen bee," while her friends were seen as "drones." She was normally the one whose parents had the most money or the most influence. In some cases, she was the most promiscuous one or the one who had no true parental structure at home, meaning, she could go out and stay out all hours of the night. (Note: I'm only talking about the not-so-good cliques, not the ones that were about education. Not all of these cliques were bad.) She could do whatsoever she desired to do, and this made her appear to be adult-like to the other students. These cliques were normally comprised of three to five women. In high school, most of these women peaked. Most people in their mid-thirties and over can confidently attest to this. And because they peaked in high school, these young women oftentimes spend the rest of their lives reliving their high school experiences. But what's both beautiful and constricting about these cliques is their loyalty to their queen bee. Most of the women remain friends for the remainder of their lives, and again, this can be good if they are all growing, learning and breaking through the membranes of information to enter new seasons. But this can be tragic when their loyalty to the queen bee hinders their growth. In other words, they won't go any further than she has because of their admiration and their appreciation of her. Now, imagine had Oprah Winfrey, for example, gotten caught up in one of those cliques. Imagine if she'd been a drone. She would have been chained to that season of her life for the rest of her life! She wouldn't be the success story that she is today, and while I am confident that she felt rejected, overlooked and judged, I am also confident that God intentionally hid her behind whatever it was that caused people to reject her, whether it was her skin color or the fact that her parents were poor. The point is, people who are designed to dominate or reach the heights of success are oftentimes acclimated with rejection. And they had to learn to be okay with this. This is how God hid Jesus. Jesus wasn't someone who looked appealing to the human eye. Isaiah 53:2 confirms this; it reads, "For he shall grow up before him as a tender plant, and as a root out of a dry ground: he hath no form nor comeliness; and when we shall see him, there is no beauty that we should desire him." You weren't going to come to Jesus because of how God arranged His facial features! You had to come to Him because you wanted the Word!

One of the mistakes we've made in the Earth is we've villainized the people like the popular girl and boy cliques in school, not realizing that everyone has his or her hour to shine. This hour isn't chronological; it's a series of events that take place once we have embraced a new heart and a new mind; in other words, a new mindset. But the villainization of people from seasons' past oftentimes causes us to get trapped in two webs:
1. Unforgiveness

2. Vengeance

So, we find ourselves laughing at the girl who was voted Most Likely to Succeed when we see her ten and twenty years later at a class reunion with five children and a beer gut. We parade ourselves around the balding former quarterback player, scoffing away when we see how bad his life turned out to be. When we do this, it simply means we're still stuck in the mindset or the season we were in when we were high school students! This means that we are still students of that particular season! To be stuck in a season is called unforgiveness! You see, in every season, there are people that you owe apologies to, and there are people who owe you a few apologies. Oftentimes, we don't get these apologies, so we can either stay stuck and wait for life to hand them what we believe they are deserving of or we can forgive the debt! Nevertheless, it is vengeful thinking to sit around and wait for someone to get the repayment you feel they deserve for their deeds! Whatever a man sows, that shall he also reap. If that person is wrong, he or she will eventually have to reap the fruit of his or her choices, but we don't have to be around to see this. As a matter of fact, when you forgive and you enter a new season, you enter a new perspective. So, a person you looked up to and felt rejected by in the last season may turn out to be someone you pray for and have compassion for in the next season! This isn't because he or she deserves your love and your pity, it's simply because God took you higher, and when you stood on that new level, you were able to see that individual from a different vantage point. For example, after high school, I started meeting and befriending women from all walks of life. Some were former prom queens, some were former strippers, and others were once considered nerds. This is why my Wise Her Still series is so popular. It's a marriage of fiction and nonfiction; in the book, I was able to write stories from so many perspectives because I've literally met people from many walks of life. Again, I've been close friends with women who felt as if society had given them a bad hand and a bad reputation, and I've been close friends with women who genuinely felt like they should have been further in life for no reason other than how they looked. And I loved both groups the same! I was able to help some of the not-so-popular girls understand society and how to overcome their shallowness, and I was able to help some of the popular girls understand society and how to overcome their shallowness! It was the same message in a different bottle! And of course, I've been close friends with balanced people. I often teach women that their beauty or lack thereof can easily become their stronghold. If they think that they are unattractive and unworthy of God's best, they may end up living a life of mediocrity, never truly reaching their full potential. If they think they are superior to other women because of their beauty, they can easily end up experiencing the taste of a good life, only to have it snatched from them every time the men who are financing their lifestyles grow bored with them and decide that they are ready to upgrade. I've seen it happen both ways! So again, you shouldn't villainize people for not allowing you or inviting you into their circles. Just understand that in every pocket or season, you will come across cliques, and if God doesn't want you married to that season, you will likely experience a lot of rejection while you're there. Don't get mad at the folks who refuse to embrace you. I love the way Apostle Paul summarizes this; in 1 Corinthians 2:8, he said, "Which none of the princes of this world knew: for had they known it, they would not have crucified the Lord of glory." God will blind folks to your potential to protect you from being accepted in the wrong season!

Transitioning

You don't come out of a season because "it's your time." Again, we've got to get past the belief, the ideology and the theology that we are waiting on a certain date and a certain hour because it's making people passive in their own growth and deliverance! You have to outgrow a season by eating and processing the information presented to you in that season. This doesn't mean that it'll be handed to you. Most times, you have to pursue new revelation. As you consume new information, it goes through your mental digestive tract; this is called your understanding. Your understanding is like a cocktail of information; it is the knowledge you have, mixed with your experiences and what you've taken from those experiences. All of these have mixed together, hardened and created your understanding. Information is filtered through this digestive tract, and then, it passes out of your life through two openings: your mouth or your choices. If it stinks in the nostrils of God, you have to stay in that season until you get the healing and the information you need to properly process that information. God is not just waiting on you to do what He told you to do, He's waiting on a certain scent! This is why the Bible says in 2 Corinthians 9:7, "So let each one give as he purposes in his heart, not grudgingly or of necessity; for God loves a cheerful giver." When obedience partners with the wrong attitude, it produces a foul odor called religion. If obedience partners with the right attitude in the right season, it produces a sweet odor called faith. If the information you've consumed passes through your digestive system and the scent rises up as sweet worship, you will find yourself advancing through that bubble, pocket or season until you reach the end of it. At the end of every given season, there is a membrane that separates each season. Some of the people walking or agreeing with you won't be able to cross this membrane, which is why some of them will attempt to sabotage you. (Note: This information is only for the folks who plan to advance out of the bubbles their parents birthed them in and reach the heights or the peaks of God's plans for them.) At the edge of every season, you'll likely experience fear, offense and maybe even trauma. The trauma isn't necessarily done to you, but it's more so done for you. It's the effects of you pushing up against the membrane of a new season. That membrane will transform your character to fit into the new region of thought that you're entering. And it sounds poetic and simple, but it's similar to entering into the Earth's atmosphere from space. The majority of objects that enter into the Earth are destroyed as they pass through the membrane or the gases surrounding the Earth. As we cross from one season into another, there is a huge temptation to stay behind. This is because of the fear that comes from leaving behind the people who you once thought you'd have around for the rest of your life (best friends, insignificant others, co-workers, etc.). We even experience the offense that comes from watching those same people attempt to sabotage us or, at most, punish us for outgrowing that particular season. Now, don't get me wrong, some people will celebrate you because they too are advancing. So, they won't necessarily go out of your life; your relationship with them may simply transition, for example, someone who was once your best friend when you were in your last region of thought can become a distant friend. Nevertheless, it is possible for the two of you to remain friends. It's no different than if two people were best friends in high school, but they ended up going to colleges that were hundreds of miles apart. They may not have the time to talk everyday or catch up with one another often, so their friendship doesn't end. It simply transitions. At some point, they may come together again as best friends, but in some cases, they will either remain distant friends, acquaintances or they will outgrow one another.

Resisting Temptation

In every region of thought, there is what we call temptation. You will come across people who you are romantically attracted to. This is not uncommon. Men and women have actually married and had babies with folks who were seasonal fixtures in their lives because they assumed that they'd be permanent or that they could make them permanent. There is a temptation to settle down in these regions of thought and there is a temptation to invest in real estate in these regions of thought. And when two people, for example, get married, this doesn't necessarily stop them from growing. When one spouse grows while the other stays behind, the warfare often comes from within the marriage, not outside of it. Should the couple break up, they will likely go on record saying, "We grew apart." And this is true! Sometimes, we meet people who've peaked while we are yet still growing!

Satan doesn't necessarily know the heights that we're called to, after all, he is not all-knowing like YAHWEH, but he does recognize a call on our lives. All the same, he knows the prophetic words that were spoken over some of our ancestors, so he will stop at nothing to ensure that those words don't come to pass. He's managed to clog up or constipate the lines between Heaven and our family members for generations, and he's trying to keep those lines from opening up for us as well! So, as we pass through each region of thought, he utilizes a method of warfare called temptation. But here's the thing about temptation—it is pointless to tempt someone with something that they are not hungry for! This means that Satan familiarizes himself with your voids. If you are anxious for anything, he will use that desire to ensnare you. A season can easily become a prison if you don't leave it in the space of time that God purposed for you to leave it. This is called a stronghold. It's when the membranes of a particular season harden, thus, making it difficult for you to escape that season. This hardness is called pride; God also refers to it as hardheartedness. Satan knows this, so he will work tirelessly to ensure that you settle down and create a comfort zone in whatever season you're in. A comfort zone is just a beautifully decorated cell. It's a place where your basic needs are met at the expense of your purpose.

As you venture through a particular region of thought, you will be met with many temptations. There's a temptation to get offended, there's a temptation to go into sexual immorality, there's a temptation to partner with the wrong people (spiritually, romantically or platonically), there's a temptation to take a seat or a throne in that region of thought and there's a temptation to quit. Of course, this is not a complete list of temptations, but these are some of the most common ones. The temptation to take a throne or a seat of authority in that season can come in the forms of:

1. **Flattery:** Flattery is oftentimes a trap. Don't misunderstand me. Compliments are great, but flattery is manipulation through the use of compliments. If enough people flatter you, you can easily find yourself feeling connected to and indebted to those people. Because of your fear of feeling or appearing to be ungrateful, chances are, you could easily fall into the trap of false loyalty. False loyalty or misplaced loyalty, according to Wikipedia is, "Loyalty placed in other persons or organizations where that

loyalty is not acknowledged or respected; is betrayed or taken advantage of. It can also mean loyalty to a malignant or misguided cause."

2. **Acceptance:** Let's go back to high school. You were rejected, albeit, not outright, by a clique of girls who only allowed blondes with college funds in their circle. You're a brunette who had to apply for financial aid. These girls are friends with you on Facebook, and one day, you receive a message from the leader of that clique. She says to you, "Hey, it's nice to see you! I'm so proud of your achievements! Keep making Jane Doe High School look good, girl! Next time you're in town, we gotta hang out!" Now, remember, the goal is to not be angry with her because she's peaked, but at the same time, you have to recognize what we call motives. What motivated her to reach out to you? Could it be the fact that you're about to graduate from law school? Could it be the fact that you're about to marry a doctor? Sudden acceptance is oftentimes a snare. Your best bet is to thank her for her kind words and show the love of God to her. Sure, you can go to lunch with her, just don't allow your rejection to bow down to her invitation. Be kind, but keep moving!

3. **Dependency or Co-Dependency:** To understand this pointer, let's think of the narcissist. A narcissistic mother buys a new car for her recently engaged son. She knows that he's recently graduated college, and neither he nor his fiance can afford new cars.

Because she fears that his new fiance will take her place, she designs the perfect scheme—have her son to get a new car he clearly cannot afford, and co-sign on that car with her son. The son falls into the snare, and before long, he finds himself having to choose between his mother's affection and his new car versus his fiance. The season for his mother to be his caretaker ended, but because of her need for control and her fear of rejection, she illegally extends that season, thus, ensnaring her son to another five years of bondage. In every season, you will find people trying to yoke themselves up with you and hold you in that season using an event called co-dependency. This is a form of idolatry, and it is a weapon designed by the enemy to keep you from moving past the season you're in.

The formula to get past temptation is a nasty one; it is one that most people have rejected or will reject because it is unpalatable to the soul. This formula is called contentment, and while we all have it in the storage space that is our hearts, most of us never partake of it. This is because we allow the enemy to burden us with fantasies; we keep watching the commercials that play in our heads, and when we don't cast these images down, they become goals. This is why you'll notice on social media that people will hashtag a photo of a couple, for example, as #couplegoals, not realizing that what they are seeing is far beneath God's plans for them. This is also why 1 Corinthians 2:9 says, "But,

Understanding Rejection

as it is written, 'What no eye has seen, nor ear heard, nor the heart of man imagined, what God has prepared for those who love him.'" Our greatest fantasies are but snippets of what God has planned for us! And this is why Satan will always offer us a settlement whenever he realizes that we are about to win or receive everything he's stolen from us and our families. It goes without saying that the cure for temptation is contentment. You must be content with God alone; any other appetite is called a void. And please note that you don't have the ability, the wherewithal or the tools to fix or fill someone who's empty; that vacancy in the individual's heart is a space that should only be occupied by the Most High God, and he or she has to invite the Lord into that space. Otherwise, you'll ignite the vacuum effect in your attempt to fill that void. Again, the vacuum effect is an attraction between one or more voids; it is a magnetic pull between one or more people that is triggered based on a need or a desire. For example, Rebecca Schaeffer was a 21-year old actress at the time of her death. She was killed by a crazed stalker named Robert John Bardo who had been stalking the actress for three years. His romantic obsession with her was completely demonic. All the same, it was based on a void. Voids create attractions; these magnetic pulls draw people to us and repel people from us. A person who is demon-possessed and mentally ill is filled with voids, and anytime a person is riddled with voids, that person will instinctively look for void-fillers. Oftentimes, these void-fillers are other people, but no human being has the capacity, the strength or the authority to fill a void. It's simply impossible.

What this means is that Robert John Bardo would have killed Rebecca Schaeffer regardless of whether or not she gave into his advances. Of course, she didn't know the guy, but the point is—he killed her because of his obsession with her. She'd been cast in a movie scene lying in the bed with another actor, and this angered her stalker. Now, if she had known the guy, dated the guy and married him, he still would have killed her. Yes, even if she'd given up her acting career. This is because what was in him was after her life. It's that simple. Mr. Bardo's obsession was triggered by rejection, the fear of rejection and a host of other issues. And anytime a person who is filled with voids fixates on another person, it is because he or she genuinely believes that the other person has what it takes to make him or her happy. This fixation can lead to fantasies, and these fantasies often lead to obsession. Obsession triggers false love, fear, anxiety, adrenaline and dopamine, as well as a host of emotions and hormones. This takes away the obsessed person's peace. Anxiety causes the individual to experience the effects that we commonly refer to as "falling in love." These symptoms include sweaty palms, a racing heart and the "butterflies in the stomach" feeling. Consequently, the obsessed party's appetite and sleeping patterns are affected. Unable to control his or her feelings, the obsessed person pacifies his or her demons by constantly monitoring the life of the person he or she is obsessed with. This only intensifies his or her obsession with the individual. This can and often does lead to the obsessed party feeling as if he or she is in a relationship with the other person, and this leads to individual to feel possessive and even jealous regarding the object of his or her affections. This is the same exact feeling that people experience when they "fall in love" with other (willing) people! Again, the sweaty palms, racing heart and queasiness of the stomach are all alarms, but we've romanticized them so much that we actually embrace them. These alarms signal that something has entered our hearts or is entering our hearts! Don't get me wrong—whenever we do begin to experience the blossoming of true romantic love, we often experience what scientists and medical professionals refer to as the "honeymoon phase." This is simply a series of emotions that have been triggered by what we know and don't know about a person. In this phase, the object of our affections appears to be nearly perfect. What makes this phase so powerful is the unity displayed during this time. There is something in unity that triggers an extreme emotional and spiritual response between two people! Over time, couples tend to grow further apart because they get the knowledge of one another, but not the understanding! Remember, God told us, "In all thy getting, get understanding." Knowledge without understanding in relationships oftentimes produces division. This division serves as a void in the relationship itself, and again, voids have strong gravitational pulls. This is how the infamous other woman or other man enters the scene. This is also why most men, whenever they cheat, have little to no plans to leave their wives. They are looking for void-fillers to fill the empty spaces in their hearts or their relationships. Women, on the other hand, often cheat with the intent of leaving. This is because of how both genders process stimuli.

The point of it all is this—every region of thought or season has potholes and pits that are designed to ensnare us. The closer we walk to these traps, the more likely we are to be pulled in by them. This is why we have to be content with God alone! The greatest temptation that we all have to overcome in every region of thought is the almost unquenchable desire to fit in and be accepted by the people who've mastered those regions of thought. But remember, if we're not in the Promised Land of our purpose, we are in the wilderness! The only relationships built in the wilderness are between predators and prey. This is why we have to repeatedly overcome rejection, fear of rejection, loneliness and all of the bruises and cuts that we get while in transition. Our goal is to chase God until He reveals Himself in us and He reveals Himself through us. This is what allows us to meet ourselves and embrace our God-given identities. Our authority is directly connected to our identities. This authority allows us to reach or take possession of every promise that God has put away for us. Sadly enough, many prophetic people die in the wilderness because they never learn to get past the guarding spirits of fear, false justice, rejection, pride and offense. But this doesn't have to be our stories. We can move from season to season until we finally step into who we are in Christ. This is where we'll find the whole armor of God; this is what allows us to freely and confidently turn around and travel back to the seasons we've overcome and lead others to freedom. This is called ministry and it's what we're all called to do.

The Shape of a Season

Your soul is the shape of the season that you're in. Remember, a season is not just a time-span or a time-stamped event; it is a pocket of information within a time-span. It is a set of beliefs, expectations and goals that have merged together to create your reality. In other words, your mind, will and emotions have been formed by your mindset or belief system. Your mindset is what you've set your mind on or based your beliefs on. In order to escape a season, you have to be transformed by the renewing of your mind; this is your mindset or belief system. What you've come to believe has to be challenged, and a lot of it has to be dislodged and denounced. Your belief system is changed one word at a time, one sermon at a time, one argument at a time or one book at a time. These are the many pressures that we all experience as we come to the truth in every area of our lives. If we discover, for example, that our best friends are really enemies disguising themselves as friends, this puts pressure on our souls. Please note that the shape of your soul is called your character (Apostle Bryan Meadows). When we come to realize that the career paths we've chosen are not the ones God has chosen for us, this puts pressure on our character. When we find out that the men or women we've been dating are untrustworthy, this puts pressure on our character. The deformation of character as the result of a negative or traumatic event is called unforgiveness. The formation or transformation of your character as the result of a traumatic event is called growth. A deformed soul cannot fit into the mold of the next season or the next region of thought. Consequently, we'd have to remain in the seasons we're in until we allow God to transform us by the renewing of our minds. And as we cross the membrane, boundaries or barriers of the next season, we can feel the pressure on our minds; it feels a lot like anxiety.

Every season is going to put pressure on you because we're constantly having to pair up or partner with people who are in different seasons of their lives, and some of them bring what the Bible refers to as "contrary winds." Matthew 14:24 reads, "But the ship was now in the midst of the sea, tossed with waves: for the wind was contrary." This simply means that the ship or vessel was heading in one direction, but the wind was pushing it in the opposite direction. In other words, the winds were working against the advancement of Jesus and His disciples. This is what we call warfare. Warfare is a strategic attempt to drive you outside the will of God. When a bunch of contrary winds come together, they form tropical storms, tornadoes and hurricanes. These storms bring destruction and chaos with them wheresoever they go. And get this, not all pressure is bad pressure. If I'm moving in the wrong direction, the contrary wind that I feel is called God's love. He's trying to push me back into His will, but He won't force me there. His winds are more like loving breezes that meet us in the noonday when we're strolling towards our mailboxes or just taking a walk around our neighborhoods. If

The Shape of a Season

I allow myself to be bent, formed and moved by His winds, my soul will start experiencing what we call transformation. But if I move against His winds, my soul will continue experiencing what we call deformation and/or conformation. If I'm in the wrong shape, I can't enter the next season!

Let's revisit the story of Tamar. Again, Tamar's soul took the shape of her trauma; the same is true for her brother, Absalom. His sister's rape negatively impacted the shape (condition) of his soul. Eventually, his wrath got the best of him. He killed his brother, Amnon, and then tried to take the kingdom away from his father, David. Because of this, he got stuck in the wrong season and ended up paying for his choices with his life.

2 Samuel 18:9-15: And Absalom met the servants of David. And Absalom rode upon a mule, and the mule went under the thick boughs of a great oak, and his head caught hold of the oak, and he was taken up between the heaven and the earth; and the mule that was under him went away. And a certain man saw it, and told Joab, and said, Behold, I saw Absalom hanged in an oak. And Joab said unto the man that told him, And, behold, thou sawest him, and why didst thou not smite him there to the ground? and I would have given thee ten shekels of silver, and a girdle. And the man said unto Joab, Though I should receive a thousand shekels of silver in mine hand, yet would I not put forth mine hand against the king's son: for in our hearing the king charged thee and Abishai and Ittai, saying, Beware that none touch the young man Absalom. Otherwise I should have wrought falsehood against mine own life: for there is no matter hid from the king, and thou thyself wouldest have set thyself against me. Then said Joab, I may not tarry thus with thee. And he took three darts in his hand, and thrust them through the heart of Absalom, while he was yet alive in the midst of the oak. And ten young men that bare Joab's armour compassed about and smote Absalom, and slew him.

Again, Absalom got stuck in the wrong season. Let's look at some of the symbolism in the story above. The mule (donkey) is a stubborn animal. Him riding on it was symbolic of his pride and stubbornness. Whenever you see trees in the scriptures, they are used to symbolize people. Different types of trees represent different types of people. This is why the blind man, after being touched by Jesus, said "I see men as trees." Of course, Jesus then touched him again. Oaks are used to symbolize strength and endurance because of their stability and longevity. The oak trees in this story represent David and his allies. David's network was strong because he had God backing him. The head represents authority. Absalom's authority had no legal standing because he'd usurped it from his father, King David. His head got caught up between Heaven and Earth, meaning, Heaven didn't recognize or acknowledge his power, so Earth could not recognize or respect his power. The mule went away, meaning, like him, the animal had no loyalty to its master. Absalom's head (authority) getting stuck is symbolic of him being unable to move forward. Because of his bitterness and ambition, he got stuck in a season and ended up paying the ultimate price for his rebellion.

Can you imagine what this must have done to his sister, Tamar? Nevertheless, in order to escape that season, Tamar would have to forgive her brother, Amnon, for raping her. She likely had to forgive her father for sending her into such a wretched situation and then, not handling the event properly. This is to answer the question—who do we blame when our parents or guardians fail to protect us, but instead, are guilty of placing us in harm's way? There's both a hard truth and an acceptable truth to this question. Let's start with the acceptable truth. You can blame your parents because they put you in harm's way, but after blaming them, you have to forgive them. Next, there's the hard truth and that is, you can blame the enemy (Satan). Our parents, guardians and leaders are imperfect, and Satan will use whatever blindspots he can find to get them to "drop the ball" in regards to us, but they weren't being malicious. In some cases, they weren't even being negligent. They just made an unwise choice. For example, King David wasn't being malicious when he sent his daughter, Tamar, into Amnon's room. He just assumed that he was doing the right thing. Now, afterwards David made the mistake of not prosecuting his son, and I believe this is where the issue became a prolonged one. He loved his children, and sometimes, a parent's love or compassion for his or her child can put the child in harm's way. I've seen this in my own family. I've seen parents giving their children everything but the discipline they needed to succeed. I've also seen the grown-up version of those children; they grew up to be rebellious, emotional, unstable, co-dependent, narcissistic and unwise.

But why blame the devil, after all, isn't that what most religious people do? They relegate the responsibility to an invisible force in their attempts to avoid taking responsibility for their own actions, right? Truth! We do see this a lot in church, but again, every leader has blind-spots, just like David had blind-spots. This is why leaders have armor bearers. Armor bearers don't just carry the pastor's Bible and water, they carry their hearts. Armor bearers protect their leaders physically, mentally, emotionally and spiritually. Armor bearers also protect their leaders' reputations. For example, all leaders are human; they may be anointed and appointed, but they are still human. Everyone knows that there are people who come into churches hoping to ensnare the pastor, and get this, they are not always wearing fitted red dresses and six-inch stilettos. They don't always have beady eyes and sultry voices. Sometimes, they look and sound sweet, innocent and harmless. Sometimes, they have puppy-dog eyes and child-like voices. If Satan does disguise himself as an angel of light, who are we to think that he doesn't put disguises on his children and those who are willing to partner with him? And these people aren't always malicious; sometimes, they genuinely believe that they can manage themselves around their leaders, even though they clearly have ulterior motives. An armor bearer needs to be able to recognize their eyes, their movements and their

The Shape of a Season

patterns; this way, they can protect, at minimum, their pastors' reputations. Again, we all have blind-spots, regardless of how anointed we are, and this is why we need people around us who genuinely love and want the best for us because the devil will attack whomsoever he can to get to you. Yes, you! This is especially true if you have an anointing to destroy his kingdom. Think of Tamar. Satan's eyes weren't necessarily on Tamar, after all, Satan thinks in generations. He had his eyes set on two of David's sons; they were Amnon and Absalom. He wanted to destroy David's lineage because he knew that Christ would likely come from that bloodline, so he put weight on Amnon's character; this weight is called obsession. He provoked and seduced Amnon with an overwhelming, unquenchable lust towards his sister, and then, he strategically ensured that Amnon would have an ungodly man speaking into his life by the name of Jonadab. Jonadab fueled Amnon's lust and gave validity to his entitlement, making him feel as if he deserved to enjoy a night with his sister with no commitments or obligations to her thereafter. Amnon was clearly a rich, spoiled narcissistic brat with rejection issues. He'd raped his own half-sister, and then, after the act was done, his feelings toward her shifted. Suddenly, he hated her. Of course, learning about this enraged Tamar's full-blooded brother, Absalom, and eventually, Absalom's heart towards his brother and his father had grown dark. He killed Amnon and ultimately set out to kill his own father. But my question is—did Tamar get justice in this? No. She lost her brother Absalom as the result of this horrid act. The point is, in a case like this, the best remedy is to heal and forgive. I have lived long enough to say that the offender will eventually reap what he or she has sown, after all, the law of sowing and reaping is immutable.

Absalom's soul had taken on the shape of rejection, trauma, hatred, bitterness and the like. When it was all over and done with, he'd taken the shape of a murderer. We're like clay. This is why we should remain in the hands of our Creator God, who is our Potter. But when hurt, anger and unforgiveness causes us to fall into Satan's hands, he starts deforming us to become whatever it is that he has decided that we should be. And after a while, Satan's plans for us become painfully clear if we'll only pay attention! His plan for Absalom was to turn him into a bitter murderer and ruler who would go against God's will and possibly operate as a narcissistic ruler over God's people! Absalom wanted his father dead! He wanted his brother dead! And if he hadn't been stopped, his murderous ways would have only gotten worse because whatever you feed will grow, but whatever you starve will die. This is the nature of a void! There is no way to satisfy or appease it. It keeps saying, "More, more, more!" At some point, it is possible that he would have looked at his sister, Tamar, and decided that she was better off dead than she was alive! He didn't just murder Amnon because of what Amnon had done to his sister; Absalom murdered Amnon because Satan had seduced him over the border of sanity, and from there, Satan had deformed his thinking.

The Shape of a Season

Blame doesn't solve a problem; it simply points it out. This is especially true if the accused chooses to defend himself or herself. For example, most therapists and counselors would advise you to confront your mother if she's been neglectful or they'd advise you to confront your father if he was abusive. But they would also tell you to go to the meeting with no hope of resolve intact. In other words, don't go there expecting that particular parent to own up to his or her mistakes. Don't expect that parent to apologize. Expect him or her to be defensive, argumentative and prideful. And if you can't handle this, they would advise you to write a note to that parent and either mail it to him or her or throw it away after writing it. This is so you can release whatever burden you're carrying. But after this, you absolutely have to take responsibility for what's currently going on in your life. You can't keep shifting the blame to your parents or the people who've negatively impacted your life in some way. If you do, you will never fully heal. Instead, you will continue to stretch the problem out, pointing out details that you didn't initially notice, thus, constantly reliving the event. In other words, blame will put pressure on your soul until you finally become a professional victim. Professional victims, by default, attract narcissists; they attract the predatory type. They can be found saying things like, "I don't know why I keep attracting the same type of guy" or "It seems like only crazy people are attracted to me! Is there some type of sign on my forehead that says, 'Hey, if you're crazy, I'm your guy!'" What they don't know is we attract people, not just based on where we are, but what we are. A man with an Ahab spirit will automatically attract a woman with a Jezebel spirit. Another way to say this is, an empathetic man will automatically attract a narcissistic woman, and vice versa. A victim or, better yet, someone with a victim's mentality, by default, is attracted to predatory types, and predators are attracted to victims. This is the spiritual food chain that most people are unaware of! This is why we should fight against the pressures of unforgiveness, blame, anger, and every other negative pressure that we experience in any given season. Those pressures can deform our souls, thus, making it difficult for us to enter into the next chapter or season of our lives.

The season that you're in represents the mindset that you currently have. One of the greatest misnomers in Christianity is that we're waiting on God for whatever it is we've been praying for, but the truth of the matter is, there's a particular shape our souls must have in order to receive the answers to our prayers. God's promises are yes and amen; in other words, He has agreed to give us the desires of our hearts; that is, whenever those desires don't serve as contrary winds to His will for our lives. For example, if I ask for a husband while I'm in the shape of a pervert, God's promises are yes and amen, however, because of where I would be if that were the case, I could only attract perverted men. This is the marriage of the minds; two cannot walk together except they are in agreement (see Amos 3:3). It is not God's will for me to be with a perverted guy, so God would send me a way of escape; this is an opportunity, a window or a space in time

The Shape of a Season

for me to escape the mindset that I'm in. He'd send mentors or random strangers to speak into my life. If I receive the counsel, my soul would begin to take on another shape. If I neglect or reject the counsel, I will cause the answer to my prayers to be delayed. Consequently, I could be found somewhere saying, "I'm waiting on God for my husband," but this wouldn't be entirely true. God's promises are yes and amen, so I'm not the one who's waiting! For example, my mother purchased a Ouija board when I was 15-years old. Not long after she purchased this board, all hell broke loose in our house. We ended up meeting a woman wearing what looked like a nun's uniform. That woman was a random stranger who'd come to our house to have her taxes done. When she saw the Ouija board, she explained to my brother and I why our family was in such chaos. She'd spoken truth into my life, and then, I never saw her again. She'd helped my brother and I to understand that Ouija boards are evil and that we were not communicating with the dead, but were instead communicating with devils. In other words, another imprint was made on my soul that day, and while it may not have been major, it was beneficial.

Consider clay. It has to be in an air-tight container in order for it to retain its malleability. You'll also notice that clay takes the shape of the container it's in UNLESS it is smaller than that particular container. If I ordered clay or purchased clay from a store, it would come in a container and it would likely take up most of that container's capacity. If I took the clay out of its container and shaped it into a rabbit, it would retain its

The Shape of a Season

shape. I wouldn't be able to get it back into that container unless it was smaller than the container. So, in essence, I will have evicted the clay from its container by simply changing its form. Another way to say this is, I would change the season that clay was in because of the pressure I put on it. And get this, even though I shaped it like a rabbit, this doesn't represent its full potential. I simply showed the clay one thing that it could become, but if I don't place it back in its container, the air will cause the clay to begin to harden. Consequently, that clay structure could potentially and permanently become a hard-headed rabbit. If someone took that clay from me and decided to put it back in its bucket, they'd have to:

1. Beat and break it into small pieces.
2. Pour water on it.
3. Put pressure on it until the water has penetrated every piece of the clay and the clay comes back together as one solid, but malleable, piece.
4. Put it back in its container.
5. Cover the container.

Now imagine that you're that clay. Satan is always trying to seduce you out of God's will so that he can show you one-tenth of your potential, and since he is the prince of the power of the air, he will harden your heart in that season, causing you to identify yourself one way when your potential is so much greater. I was looking at a former hip-hop group the other day; they had been very popular when I was in my early teens. I pretty much had every cassette tape that they'd ever released. But the spotlight on their lives began to dim before I turned 17 or 18; honestly, I think they peaked when I was around 15 because my last memory of them was when I was around 13 or 14. Anyhow, I happened to come across something the other day regarding one of the women from that group, so out of curiosity, I went and looked at her Instagram page. She looked great, but she appeared to be stuck. She had some videos up of a few performances she'd recently done, but she was performing old songs and wearing the same style of clothes she'd worn in the 80's and 90's. When clay hardens, it has reached its peak. From there, it becomes a solid rock. God wants us to stay in the container of His will, and He wants to reveal us when we take the shape of His plans for us. If not, we'll peak prematurely, and like this amazingly talented group, the world won't give us permission, grace or space to be anything other than what they've paid us to be! Think of some of the celebrities who've peaked in the nineties or at the beginning of the millennium! They have to sport the same hairstyles, use the same catchphrases and do the same things that they'd once done to make a buck, and even then, the world still regards them as irrelevant or washed up. This is also why it is absolutely dangerous for a person to chase success! Ambition has to be examined and contained; otherwise, it'll do to us what it's done to many of our predecessors! It would turn us into a lump of salt!

Your season is your mindset. If you're tired of doing the same things, seeing the same faces and earning the same

The Shape of a Season

amount of money, you have to allow God to take you to another region of thought. One of the issues I've noticed is that a lot of men and women don't know how to have relationships with people who are unlike themselves. Consequently, they harden their hearts in cliques, committing to being stiff-necked, unmovable and loyal to a particular season for the rest of their lives. What I've discovered is that when God wants to move us out of one season and into another, He often sends people who we cannot relate to, and sometimes, we don't want to relate to them. This is because we often have a misconception regarding their types, and by types, I mean, humans have a tendency to create "mental labels." This is because whenever there is a question, we feel like we must have an answer immediately. We're oftentimes not patient enough to wait for an answer, so we answer the questions ourselves. We often inherit a set of labels or categories that our parents and our communities shared with us. For example, if you grew up poor, you've probably heard people referring to their wealthier (not necessarily wealthy, just wealthier) and more orderly relatives as "high-minded." You've heard people saying, "They think they're better than us!" This was a label that you stored in your memory, so anytime someone had more money, more influence, more success, more friends, more favor or more happiness than you, and that person didn't necessarily open up his or her heart to you, you found yourself saying, "She thinks she's better than everybody!" Listen up—this is probably not true! It potentially could be, but in most cases, it's not! Whenever we lack information

The Shape of a Season

regarding a certain group of people, we form assumptions and those assumptions are filed under the labels we've created through experience and ignorance. I've found that the average Christian probably has ten to one hundred categories or labels that they tend to attach to people. The problem with this is, there are millions upon millions of categories available! Whenever they don't understand a person, by default, they place that person in one or more of the categories in their mental files. This allows them to file the person away and justify their behaviors toward that person. Consequently, they spend the rest of their lives surrounding themselves with people from the "accepted" label group, but when God wants to reach them, He often sends someone who is different. He sends someone who cannot be pressed down or categorized; this is because He's transformed and solidified them in their makeup, nevertheless, these people will still file those folks away (erroneously) under one of their categories. They do this not realizing that God is trying to give them the answers to their prayers. But to do this, He has to change their minds! To change their minds, He has to open their minds. To open their minds, He has to expand their capacity! To expand their capacity, He has to stretch them; in other words, they have to come outside of what they know! You see, when God places you around folks you cannot relate to, it forces you to be quiet! It forces you to listen and learn! Romans 10:17 says, "So then faith cometh by hearing, and hearing by the word of God." But how can I hear if I'm talking?! Jesus said in Matthew 11:15, "He that hath ears to hear, let him hear."

The Shape of a Season

The season you're in is the mindset that you have. This doesn't mean that we live in our brains; it means that what's in our brains often manifests itself as our realities. When you see children, just know that they are living in the mindsets of their parents! And while these mindsets may be the direct results of oppression, lack of information and dysfunction, the fact is that they are living in their parents' mindsets; that is, until they grow up. Unfortunately, they will inherit those patterns of thinking; they will take the shape of their parents' mindsets, but the good news is, they don't have to stay there. They need new information, new experiences and new revelation, but to get this, they have to come outside of themselves. They have to step outside of their comfort zones and allow themselves to be counseled, ministered to, rebuked, stretched and used. Yes, used! When God wants to use you, He has to acclimate you with being used, but not necessarily in a bad way! This means that you submit your gifts, your talents, your time and your resources to your local assemblies. And if you're not accustomed to this, you have the responsibility of getting past, not just the discomfort of being stretched, but those preconceived notions that you picked up when you allowed the wrong folks to use you. And finally, you absolutely, unequivocally and without fail have to learn to be mentored! Most folks don't know how to do this! They instinctively try to pull the mentors down to their levels; in other words, they try to relate to the mentor on the wrong plane. They do this so they can feel more comfortable and so that their mentors can appear to be more relatable, but this is error! What this looks like is:

The Shape of a Season

1. The mentor has escaped a particular region of thought by allowing God to change his or her mind. In other words, the mentor was promoted from the region of thought that the individual is in.
2. The mentor returns to that region of thought to minister to that individual; this is because God sent the mentor to do His work in that person's life.
3. The mentor tries to pull the person forward by giving him or her new information. The mentee tries to relate to the mentor; in other words, the mentee is holding the mentor back.
4. After the mentee feels he or she can relate to the mentor, the mentee loses honor for the mentor and starts referring to the mentor as a friend. In other words, the mentee has devalued and demoted the mentor in his or her life.
5. God gives the mentee space and grace to repent; after all, He's trying to give that person the "yes and amen" He promised them, but the mentee won't repent because he or she is not accustomed to having mentors. The mentee insists on keeping that person as a friend. This is also an attempt to hijack the next level on the mentee's part.
6. God delivers the mentor from the mentee OR he allows the mentee to continue referring to the mentor as a friend, but He limits their access, PLUS, He disallows the mentee from receiving the manna that the mentor was sent to deliver.
7. The former mentee remains in the same season year

after year, becoming stiff-necked and religious, telling anyone who will listen that he or she is waiting on God. The mentee watches everyone around him or her get promoted out of that season, but being stiff-necked, the mentee reasons within himself or herself that he or she is waiting on God.

8. God sends another person to help the mentee, but he or she doesn't know how to receive a mentor, so the mentee repeats the pattern and ultimately dishonors the mentor.
9. The cycle is repeated, the former mentee grows old, having mastered the region of thought that he or she was in, meaning, the former mentee eventually became a master manipulator. This is what happens when you get stuck in or master a region of thought!
10. The former mentee's children inherit the shape of their parents' thinking or, better yet, they are born in the same pocket or season that their parents once lived in. They can escape this, but they have to escape the pattern and the generational curse of dishonor.

MOVE ON

Has someone ever told you to "get over it" after you complained about something or someone? In today's culture, these words aren't just unacceptable, they are offensive. In truth, psychiatrists, counselors, therapists, pastors and even life itself will repeatedly tell you to "get over it." Now, people won't necessarily use those exact words. Instead, they'll tell you to move on, to heal, to let go, to forgive or to give it to God. These are just nice renditions of "get over it."

I love to watch *Judge Judy* because I'm fascinated with anything relating to legalities. One lesson I learned from watching her show is that you have to keep paying rent wherever your possessions are, even if you've physically moved! Let me explain it through an example. This is a common scenario on her show: a woman is suing her former roommate for the return of her deposit. She claims that her former roommate is withholding the deposit, even though she'd paid the last month's rent and she'd left her space in excellent condition. After hearing her testify, Judge Judy turns and looks at the defendant. She's ready to hear her side of the story. The defendant counters with this, "She moved out on the 31st, but she didn't come to get the rest of her things until the 14th!" Judge Judy then sits back in her chair, and it is clear, she's ready to rule on the case, but she has to give the plaintiff the opportunity to respond. "Did you

Move On

leave your things there until the 14th?" Judge Judy's eyes seem to pierce through the plaintiff. "I moved out on the 31st," the plaintiff counters, hoping to steer the conversation away from the facts. "That's not what I asked you!," Judge Judy shouts, clearly annoyed with the plaintiff's attempt to insult her intelligence. "Just answer the question! Or let me rephrase it. When did you go back and get your possessions?!" The plaintiff hesitates, realizing what's about to happen. "I was busy. I had to travel for my job! That's why it took me so long to get the rest of my things, but I took 90 percent of my possessions with me the day I moved out!" Judge Judy's lip curls slightly to the left. "Then, you don't get your deposit back!" she says. "I don't care if all you had was a toothbrush there! They're not obligated to keep your stuff! Your case is dismissed! Goodbye!" With that, the plaintiff is left shouting across the room, pleading with Judge Judy as she promptly exits the courtroom. This taught me three things:

1. Some people are still paying rent for the seasons they left because they haven't fully moved on! This is why they're broke!
2. Your former landlord or roommate can legally sell, destroy or trash your possessions if you don't move them in a certain amount of time. This is called grace or, better yet, a grace period.
3. Shouting as the Judge (God) moves out of a season that we are begging, pleading and demanding to stay in won't change His mind. Once He moves, you'd better move with Him! God will always meet you in the

seasons He's called you to, but in the seasons He's called you out of, His grace will remain sufficient for you. This is a hard saying, but it's the truth.

In every region of thought, there are hills, mountains and valleys. To get past a mountain or a hill, you have to either climb it (get over it) or move it with your faith. As for valleys or low places, you have to rise above them. In other words, don't be petty. To get over something, you have to humble yourself; this doesn't make sense to the natural mind, but elevation in the Kingdom looks like lowliness in the Earth. To be honest, humility can sometimes feel like stupidity, especially when you're having to humble yourself before people who have mishandled you and are not sorry for doing so. But the goal of humility is so that you don't take the shape of your offender. Every soul also has a shape, and remember that hurt people hurt people. Another way to look at this is, deformed people deform people. Again, every season has a shape. You have to get the information you need to forgive and move past every incident that Satan sets in place to chain you to that particular season. And it's not easy to do this! There are many pits, traps and giants in every region of thought you'll enter. Some of the deepest, darkest pits are the ones you didn't expect to fall into. This is why God says, "There is safety in the multitude of counselors." You need wise counsel to navigate through the many seasons that you enter, because in those regions of thoughts, there are many temperatures you'll have to experience. These temperatures are called emotions. For me, whenever I'm hurt, disappointed or scared, one of the temperatures I often experience is the desire to run away. It's no longer a temptation because I'm not going to give in to it anymore, but I'd start fantasizing about living in Europe, surrounded by rolling hills, not having to deal with people. And had God given me the money I wanted last year, I probably would have sold (or donated) all of my possessions, hopped on a plane and lived out this fantasy. He had to deliver me from being a runner; this was the shape I was in. I learned to stop running just by showing up to church and listening to my pastor preach. And when the temptation to run became so overwhelming that I was on the verge of giving into it, God gave me another dream. I posted about this dream on Facebook right after it happened! Here's a part of the post I shared:

> "Let them crucify you." Those words will forever echo in my heart. Last night, I dreamed that, out of all places, I was in an abortion clinic. What's crazy is, I was happy to be there. I'd reasoned within myself that whatever it was that I was carrying, I didn't want it anymore. I'd decided that I'd get it another way in another season under better conditions, but I didn't want it at that moment. I was sitting across from a friend of mine, chatting away and laughing. We were both ready to throw away the fruit of our wombs just so that we could get our peace back. That's when my phone rang. It was a woman raving about a pastor I know and how he'd just preached fire at a funeral she'd attended. The funeral had taken place in

another room at the abortion clinic. I told her how anointed he was and hung up. That's when I saw him leaving the clinic with his wife and children. I didn't bother to get his attention. I just pointed him out to my friend and turned back around. He went outside and was passing by the section we were seated in. There was a large window there and he glanced in and saw us. He then kissed his wife and asked her to wait in the car. He came back into the clinic, walked over and sat next to me. I greeted him and started telling him about the woman who'd just called me raving about his sermon. He wasn't interested in my small talk. He interrupted with, "What are you doing here?" I didn't answer. I just sat there. He then said, "Let them crucify you." In that dream, he made that statement three times because it was obvious that I'd made peace with the abortion. I'd made up my mind. After the final time, he said he had to leave, but he reiterated, "Let them crucify you." I eventually left and went to another clinic, but I felt out of place since it was empty and left. After that, I woke up.

Where did I want to run from, and where did I want to run to? I wanted to run from people. In truth, I wanted to leave the church scene. I didn't want to deal with the ups and downs that come with relationships because the downs felt awful. I'd decided that I was better off when I had been living in Florida with only one and a half friends. Yes, a half because the other woman was really a mentee who lived 17 hours away from me. I wanted to return to a season that God had delivered me from. This means that I was still paying rent in that season because I hadn't fully closed the door on it! And this reflected in my finances! It reflected in my relationships! It reflected in my thought-patterns. I started reminiscing about how much fun I'd had living alone in Florida, only showing my face whenever I went out to walk my dog, go to the store, do a photo shoot or hang out with my one friend. The pastor in the dream represented God. What I was about to abort was my God-given assignment. I was ready to return to a place of comfort and "false peace." I was ready to return to mediocrity! The pastor had come and sat next to me, and I did in my dreams what I often did in the natural. I tried to avoid having an uncomfortable conversation. I wanted to talk about what I wanted to talk about, not what I needed to talk about. Thankfully, I didn't abort my purpose. I hearkened to the voice of the Lord and allowed myself to feel some of the emotions I'd alienated a long time ago!

Every season has temperatures or emotions. The mistake I'd made was that I didn't ask for help when I was in that space. I tried to weather the storms alone, and this wasn't wise at all. I love the sun and I don't mind the rain, but I've never been a fan of thunder. This is because I've always feared thunder and lightning. Living in Florida helped me to get past this fear, and while I'm still no fan of thunderstorms, I'm no longer afraid of them. This is because I had to endure some of the worst storms in Florida; this is what helped me to see Georgia's storms as child's play. Wherever you live, you've

Move On

learned to manage yourself in the varying temperatures and weather-patterns; you had no choice. When you're in the midst of a storm, what do you do? You take cover, right? You go in the house! You won't just stand in the rain and let it drench you. No, you'll utilize your key (relationships), open your door (heart) and get under your covering (submit). The point is, whenever you find yourself in a storm, you need to get help! Utilize the relationships God has blessed you with, open up your heart, and more than anything, be sure to submit what you're feeling to your leaders or mentors (if you can't manage that storm alone).

Every season has a shape and every season has boundaries. Additionally, every season is transparent. I can see what's going on in the lives of the people surrounding me or, at minimum, what they choose to show me. And what this does for many of us is make us covet the next season. God desires that we be inspired and that we ask the people around us, for example, "How did you get to where you are?" Nevertheless, many believers are too prideful to do this. One of the reasons is because of entitlement. For example, I grew up poor and I grew up ignorant. There were people who judged me because of this, but that's just a part of life. God healed me, delivered me and prospered me after, of course, I fully surrendered to Him—not after I became Christian. I had to die to myself and sacrifice a LOT before walking into each level. Pay attention to the word "lot." Genesis 13:8 tells us a very familiar story; it reads, "And Abram said unto Lot, Let there be no strife, I pray thee, between me and thee, and between my herdmen and thy herdmen; for we be brethren." Get it? Abram had to sacrifice a Lot; he had to sacrifice his relationship with Lot, his nephew, in order to move to the next level. Please note that he had to sacrifice his relationship with Lot, not end it. In other words, their relationship had to transition. Abram was still there for his nephew; we see this in Genesis 14:14-16 after Lot had been taken into captivity. The story reads, "And when Abram heard that his brother was taken captive, he armed his trained servants, born in his own house, three hundred and eighteen, and pursued them unto Dan. And he divided himself against them, he and his servants, by night, and smote them, and pursued them unto Hobah, which is on the left hand of Damascus. And he brought back all the goods, and also brought again his brother Lot, and his goods, and the women also, and the people." So, he ended the close-knit relationship he had with Lot, but he didn't eliminate the relationship altogether because this isn't what God required him to do.

We all have a "Lot" that we have to sacrifice, and it's not easy! It was never supposed to be easy! But to get out of one season, we have to stop relating to our current seasons! People who master seasons look like celebrities because they know how to work the systems in the seasons that they're in, but the people who move on are eventually brought back to recover the folks who God had them to leave behind! This is, of course, for the folks who want to be rescued. Most of the people who become masterminds in a season won't allow themselves to be ministered to because they are in love with the seasons they're in. They serve as rulers in those regions of thought, so telling them to come out of a season where they are kings and queens, and enter into seasons where they are nobodies is like asking Bill Gates to stop by your house and fix your computer. They are dignitaries where they are; they'd have to become servants to get to where God is calling them. In other words, they'd have to serve their way out of their now and serve their way into their next! Then again, there are some slaves out there who love their slave-masters so much that they'll go out of their way to relate to you just so they can bind you for their masters! There are also some good people that you'll have to leave behind because they'll get stuck or climax in the wrong seasons. Again, leaving them doesn't mean abandoning the relationship altogether; sometimes, it simply has to transition. For example, I don't have the right to tell a married man how long he needs to make love to his wife before he climaxes; that's between him and his wife! (Unless I write a book or host a conference and they invest in it. Any other way is out of order!) I had to learn that same concept with people. As much as I want to pull them forward, as much as I want them to reach the peak of success, I can't demand that they not climax in the wrong seasons. I can put the messages up on videos, in books and in other forms of media, but they have to invest into those messages AND apply what they were taught! Any other way is out of order. If they climax in mediocrity, while I may be disappointed, I have to love them but leave them there. I cannot and will not allow "false loyalty" to force me to stay in an expired season just so I can prove myself to stuck folks! Their seasons are constipated and are struggling to spit them out! I have to move forward if I want the authority and the credibility I'll need to give them the release that they need; that is, if they want to be free! Should they want to come out, God may allow me to go back to start pulling on their potential, just like God allowed Abram to go back and pull Lot out of the mess he'd made. But I can't come back as a friend or a cousin. I have to come back as a servant of God!

In every given season that you enter, it is important that you:
1. Not climax in that season.
2. Respect the social boundaries drawn, even if you don't agree with them or understand them. Trust me, you'll understand them a few seasons later.
3. Forgive. You literally have to master forgiving people if you don't want to be mastered by people.

Social boundaries are set in place so that we can reach our full height and full potential in Christ Jesus. They are set in place in every season that we'll enter. For example, have you ever went to a public event, looked across the room at a bunch of wealthy folks and wondered what their lives must be like? Listen, they did the same thing with you! They looked across the room at you or someone like you and wondered what it must be like to not have to deal with the social pressures that they have to deal with. They wondered what it must feel like to have people around you just because they want to be there, not because they have ulterior motives. To you, they look free and happy; to them, you look free and happy. It's the matrix of the minds that we all find ourselves in. There are social boundaries in place that keep you from crossing over to where they are, but those boundaries don't keep them from crossing to where you are if they've been there before! These boundaries are what we culturally refer to as "personal space." For example, if you went to the opera and saw a well-known, wealthy couple, you couldn't just walk up to them and start chatting away. Physically, you could do this, but morally, you'd be out of place. This isn't because they are wealthy; this is because they don't know you. But if they walked over to you, because you are familiar with them, you wouldn't reject their presence. They wouldn't be morally out of place because they've been there before. Of course, you'd try to clear off a seat or two for them to sit down. Howbeit, this rarely happens. We don't get promoted by chance, we are promoted by God. This is why it is dangerous to try and promote yourself. It is dangerous to be the student, the teacher and the announcer at your own graduation. I get it. It's hard to deal with people, especially folks that we have preconceived beliefs about. So, the idea and the concept of needing a pastor or having to be mentored by someone isn't largely accepted within the Christian realm. A lot of anointed folks are wounded, so their oil is pouring out of their wounds. In other words, they are ministering, but it's coming out the wrong way! They will say things like, "These folks out here are saying that everyone needs a pastor! I haven't had a pastor in seven years and I've had more success in those seven years than I did when I had a pastor!" But what is success? True success isn't just wealth. Wealth is one of the branches on the tree of success. True success is wholeness. It means to be happy, healthy, sane and wealthy (if that's what you want). These people have money, but no peace. How is that success? But someone will say, "How can you say they have no peace?" It's obvious from their social media posts. They are always angry, talking about what's wrong (never what's right) and they are obsessed with cutting down church leadership. Why? Because some pastor hurt them OR they didn't get what they expected when they joined a church. Some people come in with unrealistic expectations. Obsession is the evidence of oppression!

And lastly, to shift or graduate from one season to the next, you not only have to respect the boundaries in those seasons, you have to love the people there. To love them means to forgive them—repeatedly. For example, through my company, I work with ministries. I can genuinely say that I've worked with over a thousand ministries. If I'm wrong, the number is within that range. So, it goes without saying that I've had to, not just learn to forgive sheep, but learn to forgive shepherds. You see, when you're dealing with folks' money, you get to see a side of them that most folks don't see. Don't get me wrong. Most of the men and women of God I've worked with were integral, but there were those who were not so integral. I didn't have a church home when I started my business, so I had to navigate that season using the mentors God had placed in my life, and I didn't necessarily talk about my issues with my customers to my mentors. I honestly didn't want to speak against God's elect. Now, there were the ones I was SURE were nowhere near saved, and I had to get wise counsel to get through those transactions, but I can honestly say that this probably happened a handful of times at the beginning of my launch. I'm very private about my business dealings. Forgiving someone in a headship position was a lot harder than forgiving a double-minded believer, even though these people were just passing through. This was because of my expectation. I didn't test the spirit, I tested the title, and got mad whenever the fruit didn't reflect what I thought I should've seen with the title. I've worked with catty, competitive women to men who battled with toxic masculinity. But here's what God taught me. Like most people, I thought to myself, "That woman won't go far because she has this problem, and she needs to resolve it!" or "That man won't go far because he has that problem and he needs a psyche evaluation!" Eventually, I realized that this was my hope (because of offense), not God's Word for them! Sure, some of them were broken and they lacked integrity, but God resolved that issue in my heart with these simple words (my own interpretation), "David was broken and he lacked integrity, but I still used him. Don't write people off just because they disappointed you. If I decide to take them higher, they won't be the way they are now. I'll burn it out of them through a process called love and discipline! You've met them in their process. I gave you the ability to see them naked. Now, cover them in prayer! I'm not finished with them yet! Pray for them and move on." If I hadn't listened to God's instructions, He would have closed off access to His leaders. He allowed me to see what I liked and didn't like; He even allowed me to see my arch-nemesis: jealousy! The hardest lesson I've ever had to learn was to love jealous, competitive people. This is because the energy or the force behind competition is a spirit called Sabotage! But I had to love them, and to love them means to understand where they are. But this was just a piece of the puzzle. I couldn't just focus on where they were, I had to think about where God was taking them or trying to take them; this way, I could effectively pray for them.

The way to love people is just to understand that whatever they're doing or have done represents where they are or where they were; it does not reflect where they're going! This is how you transition from one season to the next! You learn to meet people where they are; you learn to love people where they are! This is what will provoke you to pray for their deliverance, not just from one season, but you'll learn to pray them into their next season! Mark 15:33-39 reads, "And when the sixth hour was come, there was darkness over the whole land until the ninth hour. And at the ninth hour Jesus cried with a loud voice, saying, Eloi, Eloi, lama sabachthani? Which is, being interpreted, My God, my God, why hast thou forsaken me? And some of them that stood by, when they heard it, said, Behold, he calleth Elias. And one ran and filled a spunge full of vinegar, and put it on a reed, and gave him to drink, saying, Let alone; let us see whether Elias will come to take him down. And Jesus cried with a loud voice, and gave up the ghost. And the veil of the temple was rent in twain from the top to the bottom. And when the centurion, which stood over against him, saw that he so cried out, and gave up the ghost, he said, Truly this man was the Son of God." This is what graduation looks like! Sometimes, the people who crucify you in one season will be the very ones who qualify you for your next season! Jesus prayed for His enemies, even when He was in pain. This is how we graduate with honors, after all, in the Kingdom, you cannot graduate without honor. You have to love and honor, not just your pastors and the people who treat you well, you also have to love and honor those people who make it a point to dishonor you. It's not easy, but your next season is shaped like love, and if you don't get into shape, you won't be able to fit into it. Consequently, you'd find yourself having to deal with recycled storms in an expired season; that is, until you allow God, using the many tools of life, experience and His Word, to whip you into shape!

Changing seasons isn't easy, especially because of the social boundaries that we have to cross in order to go into our next seasons. We are always having to get past people and their opinions, but love will make you pray your way through the opposition and love your way through the storms; this way, you can become a vessel fit to be used by the King, Himself! And as you get to the edge of any given season, you will likely experience some of the heaviest storms in that particular region of thought. The storms don't just indicate that you're leaving a season; it's not always the devil trying to hold you back. Sometimes, the storm comes from demons that are in the region of thought that you're entering, and they are going out of their way to keep you where you are; they will even partner up with the demons of the season you're in just to keep you from advancing! This is when you'll experience the greatest pressure and this is when you'll likely endure the greatest betrayals, but the password to your next season is L-O-V-E! Don't get to the edge of your next, get hurt, and then end up staying there reconciling with the crabs in the bucket that Satan used to keep you from ascending! Move on and apologize later! Move on and God will heal you as you obey Him! Move on, and eventually the people who crucified your character will open up their mouths and say, "Truly, she was a woman of God!" or "Truly, he was a man of God!" Whatever they say about you, whether good or bad, is God's business! Your job is to MOVE ON!

A Note to the Empath and the Prophetic Individual

Believe it or not, Satan's most potent and effective weapon against you has been rejection. Most people who are prophetic were born into dysfunctional/broken families. And we can theorize as to why this happens, but more than likely the answer is—Satan saw the prophetic anointing on your family hundreds, if not thousands of years ago, and quite frankly, he was terrified of what your family could potentially do to him. Remember, Satan thinks in generations! Therefore, many generations ago, he found an open door. All the same, Satan looks at the family unit as a body; it has a head (leader), shoulders (a government), a body (foundation) and limbs (members). And get this—the most effective way to destroy a body is to cut off the head. Again, the head represents authority.

1 Corinthians 11:3: But I would have you know, that the head of every man is Christ; and the head of the woman is the man; and the head of Christ is God.

The head of the family unit is the husband. Satan knows this, even though this generation is trying to escape this fact. And this is largely because twenty five percent of American children are being raised in single parent households. Afro.com reports the following:

A Note to the Empath and the Prophetic Individual

"It found that a majority of the 73.7 million American children under age 18 live in families with two parents (69 percent)—a decrease from 88 percent in 1960. Of those 50.7 million children living in families with two parents, 47.7 million live with two married parents and 3 million live with two unmarried parents.

Broken down by race, however, the statistics show stark differences. The percentage of White children under 18 who live with both parents almost doubles that of Black children, according to the data. While 74.3 percent of all White children below the age of 18 live with both parents, only 38.7 percent of African-American minors can say the same. Instead, more than one-third of all Black children in the United States under the age of 18 live with unmarried mothers—compared to 6.5 percent of White children. The figures reflect a general trend: During the 1960-2016 period, the percentage of children living with only their mother nearly tripled from 8 to 23 percent and the percentage of children living with only their father increased from 1 to 4 percent."

(Source: Afro News/The Black Media Authority/Census Bureau: Higher Percentage of Black Children Live with Single Mothers/Zenitha Price)

What we have been witnessing is the removing of the head. Consider the story of David and Goliath. As soon as David killed Goliath, he decapitated him. 1 Samuel 17:51 details this event; it reads, "Therefore David ran, and stood upon the Philistine, and took his sword, and drew it out of the sheath thereof, and slew him, and cut off his head therewith.

A Note to the Empath and the Prophetic Individual

And when the Philistines saw their champion was dead, they fled." Why did David decapitate Goliath? It was a common war practice back then that served many functions:
1. It ensured that the enemy was dead. Men could survive being impaled by a spear, thrust with a sword, shot with an arrow or cut with a dagger, but no man can survive decapitation.
2. It was often used as evidence after an assassination to prove that the targeted individual was indeed dead. Carrying the dead-weight of an entire body was way too complicated. Warriors settled for just taking the head of a person.
3. It served as a trophy. Severed heads were often hung from trees; this allowed the people to see their enemies and celebrate. This also provoked fear in other nations.
4. It signifies that the war has been won or will be won. Once the men saw that Goliath was dead, they all fled in fear.

Removing the head of an individual, especially someone of notable rank represents destroying the authority of that particular individual and all that he represented. This is why Jehu not only killed Ahab's sons, he decapitated them—all 70 of them. And now, Satan has advanced into many of our parental and familial states, and from there, he has removed the father figure. The husband represents the protector, the provider and the voice of leadership. Remember, we discussed that we have multiple states to us and Satan's

A Note to the Empath and the Prophetic Individual

objective is to get into these states and bring utter destruction. He then advances against that state; that is, until he's removed the authority from that state. This allows him to advance to the neighboring state. Think fatherhood. This is a neighborhood of thinking within the parental state. What Satan has done to many of our families is, he's entered the parental state and advanced against the males in our family. He then decapitated the father-figure from the family unit. Over time, fatherlessness became normalized in many of our families. Howbeit, as common as this became, it did not stop the children from feeling the weight, the anxiety and the fears that came with not having an active father in their lives. All the same, fatherlessness isn't always the physical removing of the father-figure. In many cases, Satan just attacked the man's mind, his confidence and his authority so much so that he had no voice in his home. Or maybe his voice was perverted; maybe he was an incestuous pedophile or maybe he was plain abusive. Either way, the head of that family had been removed and this gave way to the Jezebel spirit. Again, this is what we refer to as the common narcissist. But get this—Satan's invasion of a family did not remove the prophetic anointing from that family, it simply silenced or perverted the prophetic voices that would arise from that family. Consequently, we see families who are extremely creative, talented and anointed, but their broken, twisted in their thinking and severely divided. This would mean that Satan's campaign against that particular family has been relatively successful; that is, until someone in the family rises up and decides to fight back. But in order for this

A Note to the Empath and the Prophetic Individual

to happen, the person would have to wake up, and by this, I mean, the person would have to:

1. Get to know and accept Jesus Christ as his or her Lord and Savior. And not just religiously, but intimately.
2. Chase the heart of God with everything in him or her. This means that the individual has to step outside of religion and chase the heart of God. And by religion, I mean to step outside of unprofitable, meaningless religious practices that were taught to the individual. Amazingly enough, many narcissists are incredibly religious, but they don't have an intimate relationship with the Lord. Instead, they work tirelessly to get some measure of rank in their local church assemblies.
3. Become aware of his or her identity. Referring to yourself as an "empath" is politically correct, but spiritually speaking, you just may be a prophetic individual. This is why you need a good church home, especially one that is familiar with prophetic ministry.
4. Accept his or her call into ministry. This does NOT mean that the individual in question will become a pastor or hold a religious title! It means that he or she must accept his or her God-given assignment in the Earth and begin to execute that assignment.
5. Draw boundaries around himself or herself and enforce those boundaries. The reason this is important because without boundaries, the individual will repeatedly be wounded by the narcissists in his or

A Note to the Empath and the Prophetic Individual

her family or in that individual's life.

Prophetic individuals have to acclimate themselves with rejection. Think of it this way. Imagine that your family was called to Miami, Florida 17 generations ago, but no one has ever obeyed God and moved. You finally wake up and realize who you are, and as soon as you open your ears and your heart to the Lord, He send prophets to confirm to you what He's laid upon your heart. They all say, "God is calling you to Miami." But don't think of this analogy in modern-day terms, meaning, don't think about flights and moving trucks; instead, imagine that your move there has to be on foot, and you have to travel through many neighborhoods of thinking to get there. What's worse is you live in Los Angeles, California, so your journey on foot would take you 922 hours to complete; that is 38 days. But you are required to stop in certain towns and stay there for a year. All the same, every time you leave one town, you enter into the country; this is the wilderness between two towns. So, as you journey, you have to settle down in some towns for a year or so; these are your rest stops. In some of those cities or towns, you are eager to leave because of the small-minded people who live there. Howbeit, there are some municipalities that you absolutely love! The people are great, the food is delicious and the weather patterns are perfect! So, while living in these places, you secretly wish that God would just reassign you to that place, after all, you are a long ways away from where you started. Nevertheless, like clockwork, God hands you a new map and off you go to the next city. And in every

A Note to the Empath and the Prophetic Individual

region of thought that you enter, there are beautiful people who would love nothing more than to settle down with you, and if we can be honest, you tried to settle down with a few of them. Like Jonah, you tried to hide from God because you didn't want to embrace your assignment. You may have hid in marriages, hid behind your career or even hid behind your pain. None of this works. Every hiding place of yours is illuminated every time God comes looking for you, and when this happens, the light from His presence causes you to see your perverted reality all the more; these are the issues you refused to acknowledge. Also, you've discovered that in every region of thought, most of the people are not embracing of you. You are oftentimes rejected, misjudged and looked down upon. This is because you are the student in all of these seasons, but you always get the attention of the masterminds of those seasons because of how quickly you are advancing forward. To teach you a lesson, these people either passively or directly attack your character. And this has been a pattern that you've witnessed over the course of your life. What's happening here? It's simple. You're not called to Georgia, you're not called to Texas and you're not called to Arizona. What this means is, God will allow your comfort zone to be disrupted or, in some cases, He won't allow you to get too comfortable with many of the people you meet, the jobs you get or the places you journey into. The goal is to get you to do what your family should have done generations ago; that is, move to Miami!

Of course, I'm using physical locations to describe a spiritual

A Note to the Empath and the Prophetic Individual

principle. The point is, most prophetic people have to acclimate themselves with rejection because God has to take them through so many regions of thought to get to where He's called them. This means that as soon as they get comfortable in friendships, God delivers them. As soon as they get comfortable in relationships, God delivers them. Because of this, most empaths/prophetic individuals settle down in neighborhoods of thinking that they are not called to. These regions of thought are called caves. Many of them become frustrated with God; this is because Satan keeps inundating their minds with fantasies of being normal and living normal lives. Read this carefully—if you are a prophetic individual, there is nothing normal about you! Most of the warfare that you've endured has been because you've tried to settle down in regions of thought and force God to give you a normal life, but this has always blown up in your face. You have to learn what many of your predecessors have discovered and that is—running from your calling is the same as volunteering to be swallowed up by a great fish. In Jonah's case, that great fish has been said to have been a whale, when this is not true. A great fish simply means a big fish; it could have been a whale, a huge shark or a marine animal that we aren't so familiar with these days. Either way, Jonah found himself in what could have easily become his grave. This is what happens to empaths. You may have been overwhelmed and consumed by a narcissist; this is the great fish that swallowed you when you attempted to run away from your assignment. And to get out of this fish's belly, you would have to do what Jonah did.

A Note to the Empath and the Prophetic Individual

1. He repented.
2. He said "yes" to his assignment.

Of course, Jonah was a prophet of God, and like many prophets, he just wanted to live a normal, drama-free life. But he wasn't created to be an ordinary man; he was wired to be a prophet of the Lord. The point here is this—you may be called or chosen by God to perform a specific assignment in the realm of the Earth. But the enemy to this assignment is rejection. After experiencing it so much, you may have done some silly things to avoid feeling that pain again. After all, the pain of rejection can be intense, especially when it comes from someone you love and trust. Nevertheless, rejection is sometimes a dried up brook. Sometimes, God won't bless the cities that we're in beyond our allotted time to be there. Our assignment is to get the revelation and the healing needed, and then to move on. You've experienced a great deal of rejection because you have not accepted your assignment in Christ. Maybe you don't feel like you're ready. Please note that no prophet or prophetic individual ever feels ready enough. Consequently, the very first sacrifice that he or she must give to God is his or her comfort! Fear is another enemy that must be laid on the altar and decapitated!

As you move through each region of thought, what you'll soon discover is that God is putting you back together again. He'll restore an arm, and then, a hand, followed by a finger. What you're doing is finding yourself. And the more you find yourself, the more your eyes will open to your identity and

A Note to the Empath and the Prophetic Individual

your ears will open to the voice of God. And while you are being restored, God will begin to restore your family. He'll break the generational curse of fatherlessness by allowing you to get the knowledge, understanding, wisdom and revelation needed to set your family free. If they refuse to embrace this freedom, He'll use you to start a lineage of generational blessings. This is very similar to cutting a branch off a tree and placing it in water or soil. Many farmers do this to allow the branch to grow roots. Once the branch reaches a specific size, they relocate it to the soil that they want the tree to grow in. What this means is that what was once a member of a larger body is now creating its own body. It goes without saying that most of us don't want this. We want to see our families be made whole and unified, but this doesn't always happen; this is why you don't want to over-romanticize the concept of having a normal family if they are broken, rebellious and proud. Sometimes, God will treat you like a branch and start something new from you. And while this may be painful, frustrating and lonely, it starts a generational blessing that your children, grandchildren and great-grandchildren will benefit from. In other words, your sacrifice will not be in vain. And no worries—God won't force you to do life alone (if this applies to you). He'll graft you in a family made by His own blood and rooted in His Word. Satan may have removed the head from your family unit decades ago, but God said that He would give His children a new heart and a new mind. In other words, He will give you another head; He will bring father-figures into your life who are not only sound, but they are blessed and they are stable.

A Note to the Empath and the Prophetic Individual

The short of this is—don't spend another moment crying and complaining about what you don't have. Instead, chase the heart of God so that He can fix what your great-grandparents may have broken generations upon generations ago. You got this because God's got you!

Note Center

Great day to you and thank you for reading the third installation of the Book of Boundaries. I pray that the information in this book not only opened your eyes, but that it also gave you the motivation, the insight and the tools you need to set and secure boundaries in your life. And since this is the second book in the series, I decided to create this section for you to document your progress as you navigate through each book and as you navigate through life in general. Use the space provided below to detail some of the lessons you've learned, how you plan to apply them and to journal about your success and failures. Happy boundary-building!

Your Name	
Today's Date	
City, State	

Who are your boundaries designed to protect?
- Name:
- Name:
- Name:
- Name:
- Name:
- Name:
- Name:
- Name:

Use this section to write a letter to the future you. Come back and read this letter anytime you need encouragement or to be reminded why you decided to set and enforce boundaries in your life.

Journal

CCLXXXV

CCLXXXVIII

CCLXXXIX

Printed in Great Britain
by Amazon